BLACKSTONE GAS GRIDDLE BIBLE

2000 Days of Succulent and Juicy Recipes for Your Blackstone to Unlock your Inner Grid Master. Tips and Tricks for Exceptional Cooking.

Liam Walker

TABLE OF CONTENT

INTRODUCTION

The outdoor gas griddle is a versatile kitchen appliance that can be used year-round and in any climate. It is designed for outdoor use, with a durable grill top and cast-iron body. With excellent heat retention, you can cook foods faster than on a traditional stovetop and reduce your carbon footprint. It is also for people who are on the go and want to prepare meals ahead of time, saving time and energy when entertaining.

It provides excellent cooking efficiency. It utilizes new technology, in which the heat source is circulated from the bottom of the griddle to the top, unlike other griddles that use solid walls for insulation. This excellent heat retention allows your food to cook evenly without burning and preserves energy. In addition, the cast-iron design provides exceptional durability, with a large surface area compared to typical griddles. This translates to less time spent cleaning and more time enjoying your food.

The outdoor gas griddles are built and designed to allow easy cleaning, so you do not need to worry about using too much time cleaning up the stove. It has a smooth surface that makes it easy to wipe clean with an ordinary cloth. It also has a convenient grease spout that aids in transferring the grease from the stovetop directly into a container.

Since it has been designed for outdoor use, with durable construction and a protective grill top, you will be able to use it in any climate, with the right size for any sized meal. Its dual-fuel system is also an attractive feature compared to other griddles, with the option of running on either gas or propane. When cooking w gas, add propane at the beginning of cooking and you will get an even distribution of the heat.

People can use their outdoor gas griddle for any number of purposes. Its versatility makes it ideal for camping, tailgating, boating, or backyard gatherings. It is also great for a supplemental cooking appliance; you can cook breakfast foods and lunch items with one griddle. Additionally, you can prepare multiple dishes ahead of time to enhance your menu options. This versatile appliance can save you time, money, and effort.

There are many unique things about the outdoor gas griddle that set it apart from other griddles, but there are also some basic recipes that you should try out. Then, when you decide to use this device, you can prepare various meals.

The outdoor gas griddle can be used throughout the year, with a portion of the product life cycle dedicated to each season. You will also have options for cooking on both gas and propane, depending on your needs. Both fuels provide the same cooking experience, with propane being more economical in fuel cost very use.

Enjoy the many benefits of the outdoor gas griddle and take your cooking experience to the next level. The adaptability of the griddle allows you to cook everything from classic grilled cheese sandwiches to seafood or vegetables, allowing you to have a healthier version of your favorite restaurant meals right at home.

CHAPTER 1:

SETTING UP THE GRIDDLE

Griddles are cookware designed to cook food evenly, with or without grease. They usually come in two varieties: electric and stovetop. Though the type you use doesn't matter, many people prefer a gas griddle because of its efficiency and control.

You'll need a whole lot of parts, such as a propane cylinder, regulator, igniter, and hose. The process will also require you to drill holes in the side of the grill box to install a stainless-steel vent and pipe so that the propane gas can be released while cooking on the griddle.

Finally, you'll use your grill box to install racks on the inside, which will give you more space and flexibility to cook a large amount of food.

Gas Griddle Assembly

1. Assemble the griddle. The gas griddle can be bought from most hardware or home improvement stores. Some of them come pre-assembled, while others require basic assembly. Follow the construction guide that comes with your griddle to assemble it properly.
2. Attach the regulator to a propane cylinder and connect a hose to it. The regulator will control the flow of propane gas into your griddle's fuel regulator valve.
3. Connect the igniter to the fuel regulator valve. Use a matchstick for this part and place it in a hole in the regulator. Place your igniter pins on top of this stick when you're finished.
4. Connect the igniter to the propane fueling hose by inserting it into one end of it.
5. Insert one piece of the wire into the other end of the propane gas hose and secure it into place with a wrench. Then, insert the other end of the gas hose into your griddle's fuel regulator valve and tighten it into place with a wrench.
6. Drill holes on each side of your griddle box so that you can attach vent pipes. The holes should be about 1.5" from the bottom of the griddle and about 4.5" from each sidewall of the box.

7. Attach one end of a stainless-steel vent pipe to one hole and use a wrench to attach it into place tightly.

8. Attach the other end of the vent pipe to your griddle's fuel regulator valve. Connect one end of your propane hose to the regulator and connect the other end to its output port.

9. Fill your propane cylinder with gas, use a funnel for that part, and ask a friend to help you if possible. Use long-handled garden shears to cut the hose if it is too long for you to use a wrench for this process.

10. Attach your griddle to a gas grill by positioning it over the hot coals and lighting the igniter.

Learning the Controls of Gas Griddle

In cooking, gas griddle knowledge is very important, especially when handling the heat settings. It is crucial to understand how the griddle control works so that you can cook your food correctly.

The Start Button

This button will ignite the propane gas flow to your grill box, ignite the igniter, and ignite your griddle's burner.

The Power Button

This button will turn your griddle on and off when it's in use. You should also know that this control works on both electric and gas griddles.

The Black And White Controls

These buttons are used to adjust the cooking temperature of your griddle as well as its flame's intensity.

The Timer

This is used to keep track of the hours and minutes that your griddle is cooking. The timer will also let you know when to add coal to your grill, as well as the timing needed for every step of the griddle's cooking process.

The Indicator Lights

These lights will let you know what's going on in your grill at all times and will also give you a light to see if there is electricity or gas present. They will also tell you the status of your griddle's burners, which include their flame size, heat temperature, and whether they are lit or not. This is very important as it lets you know if your griddle is working properly.

Tips and Warnings

Buy a griddle with adjustable racks with which you can raise or lower the height of your cooking surface. Keep in mind that a griddle should be placed about 6" above your burners to ensure proper ventilation during operation.

Gas griddles are heavy, so make sure they're properly set up before using them for cooking food.

1. Don't use propane gas to power anything bigger than your griddles, such as a stove or oven. The fire it creates could ignite and cause an explosion, causing injury or damage to property.

2. Don't use a gas grill on top of another grill box, which uses charcoal, or uses wood chunks to fuel it. It could result in a fire because the oil or grease from your griddle is flammable.

3. Never cook with metal utensils or any utensils with a sharp edge because they could catch fire and cause injury. Use wooden or plastic utensils to avoid this.

4. Don't put your griddle on top of broken ground, as this could lead to a fire.

5. If you're not using the grill in a gas-safe area, ensure that your regulator's hose is long enough to reach the nearest gas supply. Also, make sure that the hose isn't exposed to any moving parts or flames because they could damage it if they come into contact with it.

CHAPTER 2:

THE EXTRA ACCESSORIES THAT GIVE EVEN MORE QUALITY AND EASE

Every outdoor gas grill requires a few additional, less obvious accessories. Griddles and other cooking surfaces are a very important part of the outdoor kitchen that is often overlooked.

There are several accessories you'll want to consider adding to your gas griddle. They include:

Cover

A cover adds a new dimension to your outdoor cooking experience. It provides an extra level of protection from the elements.

Grill Plates

A set of grill plates are essential for any outdoor kitchen. You can use these plates in place of a direct heat rack when cooking with indirect heat. In addition, these plates allow the lid to close completely, creating more usable space inside the grill.

Baskets

Baskets allow air to circulate beneath your griddle or cooking surface, which will help keep food from sticking.

Table

A table can accommodate multiple pots and pans. It also serves as a place to rest your grill while it cools down.

Thermometer

A thermometer is essential when cooking with indirect heat on your gas griddle. It will keep you from overcooking your food and burning your gas. It will also help you maintain the proper temperature inside the grill to eliminate the need for guesswork.

Griddle Lifter

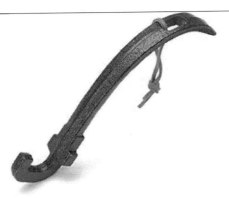

A griddle lifter makes cleaning your grill easy by lifting the cooking surface off of its hinges. It also helps protect burners when adding or removing food from the pan.

Drip Pan

A drip pan helps catch excess grease. This keeps the inside of your grill from getting too smoky and smelling up your outdoor kitchen. They also keep the outside from getting messy and making a huge mess of burnt grease.

Propane Adapter

This will ensure you always have enough fuel to run your griddle.

Some of the accessories listed above are not as important as others, but every item is essential for the proper operation of a gas griddle.

Griddle tools are also an important part of a gas griddle setup. You'll need a special tool that helps you clean your griddle and keep it in good shape. These items include:

Oil Brush

The oil brush is a small plastic tool with a rubber pad inside of it. The pad has smaller, circular pieces of sponge inside it. It will keep your griddle in good condition and protect its surface from rust.

Scraper

A scraper is a long, flat metal tool. It has a serrated edge that allows you to scrape up any food that hasn't been cooked or burned properly.

Spatula

A spatula is a long, thin tool with a plastic handle on it. One side is flat and the other is a serrated edge. It is used to move cracked food to the center of the griddle for even cooking.

Small Brush

It is a small hand-held brush with soft bristles. This brush is used to clean the griddle and dry it after washing.

Cleaner Pad

A cleaning pad is used for cleaning and scrubbing both non-stick surfaces and food stuck on one of your cooking surfaces.

Silicone Brushes

Silicone brushes are used to clean the griddle. They are long and thin, with a soft silicone coating on one side.

Spatula Holder

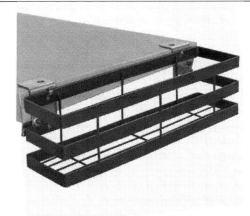

A spatula holder is like a rack that keeps your spatula from slipping and falling off the cooking surface. This will also prevent damage to the griddle from overusing it.

Paper Tower Holder

It keeps your grill clean and dry while it's cooling down. It also allows you to remove burned food from the grill grates. It is used to wipe grease and excess food from the griddle.

Rags

Rags are used to clean the griddle. They are used to clean grease or moisture from the cooking surfaces.

Barbecue Scraper

It is made of plastic or metal, with a flat edge on one side and a curved edge on the other. The flat end is for scooping debris from melted fat drippings, while the curved end is for scraping your griddle's surface clean.

Mixing Bowl

A mixing bowl is used to mix food and ingredients. You can use this bowl on your griddle as well.

Mixing Utensil

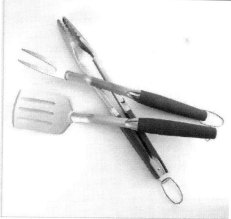

A mixing utensil is used for whipping up sauces, combining ingredients, and more. Use it to combine ingredients in your griddle or on the stovetop.

Coaster

A coaster is a small plastic or metal plate that protects your table from burning grease.

Gloves

A heat-resistant glove is a thin, disposable glove made out of silicone. They are used to handle high-temperature items without burning your hand.

All the items listed will help you cook food on your griddle effectively and efficiently. Each item has its unique purpose, and it's all about figuring out how you want to use your griddle. The more accessories you have available, the easier it will be to cook various foods on your griddle.

THE BENEFITS OF GRILLING WITH THE GRIDDLE

Griddles are a popular choice for restaurants and other establishments that need to prepare large volumes of food quickly and efficiently.

Besides cooking different types of foods, using a griddle is also a great way to grill food. You can use this if you want to prepare food without putting oil or fat on your food. It can be used by anyone, especially those who want to start a healthier diet for their children or adults.

Benefits of Gas Griddle

Cost-Effective

Griddles are a cost-effective solution for restaurants that want to serve many customers with a single cooking surface. Gas griddles can cook 30–40% more food than a standard flat top grill.

Versatile

Griddles offer a range of 12 inches to 36 inches in length. Because the cooking surface is adjustable, gas griddle owners can make optimal use of their space by customizing the size according to their business needs.

It is an option for many cooking applications because they only require electricity to run. Since they are smaller than steam or convection ovens, gas griddles are very compact and can fit into tight spaces. The gas griddle is also more efficient than conventional ovens by using more fuel and has no pre-heating requirements.

Fast Heat-Up Time

Griddles can reach 450°F within minutes, and they are ready to cook as soon as they reach temperature. Gas griddles have no waiting time for pre-heating, which helps reduce food waste.

Strong, Durable Construction

They are constructed out of heavy-duty steel that can withstand extreme conditions. They also have heavy-duty stainless-steel cooking surfaces and a durable cast iron wear plate that is easy to clean.

It Can Cook Anything

Griddles can cook anything that is placed on the surface. The cooking plate is also insulated, and therefore it can be used to cook meat, fish, and vegetable dishes without any additional pre-heating time.

Get Better Flavor from Your Food

Since a griddle cooks on the surface, it lets you get the better flavor out of your food. It can hold moisture and fat on the cooking surface. It is much easier to cook on than a flat-top grill. A griddle also distributes heat evenly.

Cook Tasty Food

You can cook fried eggs, pancakes, bacon, grilled cheese sandwiches, French toast, and so many more foods without using any grease or oil to fry them up. Instead, you can enjoy the taste of natural food ingredients uncooked but cooked at high temperatures on a gas griddle.

Faster Cooking

Griddles can cook a greater number of items without the use of any cooking oil. It is also faster to prepare food on a gas griddle than using a standard electric oven. This saves time and money, especially for businesses that are having trouble staying organized. For example, an omelet on a gas griddle cooks in less than one minute, while an omelet in an oven can take up to 15 minutes.

Cooks Uniformly

The gas griddle heats up quickly, which means food cooks evenly. It is also easier to cook food that requires high heat on a griddle. This is because the consistency of cooking temperature and the surface is the same. By using this tool, you have an even distribution of heat, and everything will be cooked at once without having to cook each piece separately, especially if you are preparing a large amount of food.

Food Doesn't Stick

Griddles have a non-stick surface, so it makes preparing foods easy. Food doesn't stick to the cooking plate; this means there is no need for you to use oil or grease to fry up your food.

Less Mess

All of the fat and grease from your food stays on the cooking plate, making it very easy to clean. Food is cooked on top of the griddle, and it doesn't splatter all over your kitchen. The grease can be easily wiped off using paper towels or a soapy rag.

Intense Heat Source

Griddles are made out of thick copper-coated steel that absorbs heat evenly, improving efficiency. The added copper also prevents the pan from rusting and makes it more durable.

CHAPTER 3:

MEAT RECIPES

1. Easy Griddle Steak

Preparation Time: 10 minutes
Cooking Time: 20 minutes
Servings: 4
Ingredients:

- 4 steaks of your choice, 1-inch thick
- 2 tablespoons olive oil
- A few sprigs of thyme
- Salt and pepper to taste
- 2 tablespoons butter

Directions:

1. Flavor the steak with a light coating of olive oil. Then, sprinkle the rest of the ingredients.
2. Preheat the griddle pan to 300°F and place two steaks at a time on the non-oiled surface of the pan.
3. Cook for 3 minutes per side.
4. Rotate the steaks to cook the other side.
5. Two minutes before the cooking time ends, add a tablespoon of butter.
6. Repeat the process with the rest of the steaks.
7. Allow the steaks to rest on a plate before slicing and serving.

2. Ribeye Steak and Mushrooms

Preparation Time: 10 minutes
Cooking Time: 30 minutes
Servings: 2
Ingredients:

- 2 16-ounce Ribeye Steaks
- Salt and pepper to taste
- 8 ounces baby Bella mushrooms, sliced
- 3 garlic cloves, minced
- 1 tablespoon fresh rosemary
- 1 tablespoon vegetable oil
- 2 tablespoons butter

Directions:

1. Flavor the steaks with salt and pepper to taste.
2. Place mushroom in a bowl and add the garlic and rosemary.
3. Turn the griddle to 300°F and preheat for 10 minutes.
4. Oil the griddle pan and cook the steak for 5 minutes on each side.
5. Flip the steaks and place foil on top to seal the heat. Do this twice so that the steak cooks for 10 minutes on each side.

6. After 15 minutes, add the butter and cook for another five minutes.
7. Add in the mushroom on the side of the griddle and cook together with the steaks.
8. Serve immediately.

3. Korean Ground Beef Rice Bowl

Preparation Time: 10 minutes
Cooking Time: 15 minutes
Servings: 4
Ingredients:
- 2 tablespoons olive oil
- ¼ cup ground beef
- Salt and pepper to taste
- ¼ cup light brown soy sauce
- ½ teaspoon crushed red pepper flakes
- 2 cups cooked brown rice
- 2 teaspoons sesame oil
- Chopped scallion for garnish

Directions:
1. Heat the griddle to 300°F and pour in the oil.
2. Cook the beef and stir until golden brown, then season with salt, pepper, and soy sauce.
3. Add in the red pepper flakes and stir in the rice.
4. Keep stirring until well combined.
5. Put sesame oil and scallions then stir for another 3 minutes.
6. Serve.

4. Griddle-Seared Kobe Beef

Preparation Time: 5 minutes
Cooking Time: 5 minutes
Servings: 6
Ingredients:
- 14 to 16 ounces Kobe strip steak
- Salt and pepper to taste

Directions:
1. Place the steak inside the fridge for an hour to solidify the fat.
2. Heat the griddle for at least 5 minutes.
3. Remove the steak from the fridge and cut it horizontally to turn them into thick strips.
4. Season with salt and pepper to taste.
5. Once the skillet is hot, sear each slice for 30 seconds per side.

5. Rump Steak

Preparation Time: 5 minutes
Cooking Time: 6 minutes
Servings: 1
Ingredients:
- 1 rump steak, 5 cm thickness
- A drizzle of vegetable oil
- Salt and pepper to taste

Directions:
1. Take the steak from the fridge and thaw to room temperature.
2. Preheat the griddle grill to 300°F for 5 minutes.
3. Splash vegetable oil over the griddle pan and cook the steak for 3 minutes on each side.

4. Massage with salt and pepper on each side.
5. Serve.

6. Hibachi Steak

Preparation Time: 30 minutes
Cooking Time: 10 minutes
Servings: 3
Ingredients:

- 2 garlic cloves, minced
- 1-inch ginger, grated
- 1 teaspoon sugar
- 3 tablespoons soy sauce
- 1 tablespoon water
- 1 tablespoon oil
- 2 1-inch-thick New York strip steaks
- Sesame seeds and scallions for garnish

Directions:

1. In a mixing bowl, put garlic, ginger, sugar, soy sauce, water, and oil. Mix until the sugar is dissolved.
2. Arrange steaks in a Ziploc and pour the marinade. Marinate for 30 minutes.
3. Heat the griddle pan to 450°F for 5 minutes. Cook for 3 minutes per side. Remove the steaks from the grill before slicing.

7. London Broil

Preparation Time: 24 hours
Cooking Time: 12 minutes
Servings: 8
Ingredients:

- 2 pounds London broil

- 1 cup dry red wine
- Salt and pepper to taste

Directions:

1. Score the meat with a fork.
2. Arrange in a Ziploc and pour in the red wine. Marinate for 24 hours in the fridge.
3. Heat the griddle pan for 5 minutes.
4. Take the meat from the marinade and flavor with salt and pepper.
5. Place the meat on the griddle and cook for 6 minutes on each side.
6. Set the internal temperature at 135°F. Allow the meat to rest before slicing.

8. Steak and Peppers

Preparation Time: 10 minutes
Cooking Time: 10 minutes
Servings: 2
Ingredients:

- 1 tablespoon olive oil
- 2 garlic cloves, minced
- 200-gram strip steaks, sliced
- 1 large yellow bell pepper
- 1 large red bell pepper
- 1 large green bell pepper
- Salt and pepper to taste

Directions:

1. Remove the seeds of bell peppers, and then cut them into short and thin strips.
2. Heat the griddle pan to 350°F.
3. Add the oil and sauté the garlic for 2 minutes.
4. Stir in the steaks and stir for 3 minutes.

5. Add the bell peppers and sauté for another 3 minutes.
6. Season with salt and pepper to taste.

9. Lamb with Spiced New Potatoes

Preparation Time: 10 minutes
Cooking Time: 20 minutes
Servings: 4
Ingredients:
- 2 tablespoons olive oil
- 1 large garlic clove, crushed
- 1 heap cumin seeds, crushed
- 8 lamb chops
- Salt and pepper to taste
- Chopped mint leaves
- 3 pounds cooked potatoes, halved

Directions:
1. Warm the griddle pan over medium heat and pour oil.
2. Sauté the garlic and cumin seeds until toasted.
3. Add in the lamb chops and sear for 3 minutes on each side.
4. Flavor with salt and pepper to taste.
5. Garnish with mint leaves and serve with cooked potatoes.

10. Easy Grilled Lamb Chops

Preparation Time: 5 minutes
Cooking Time: 15 minutes
Servings: 6
Ingredients:
- 6 lamb chops

- 2 tablespoons garlic powder
- 1 tablespoon fresh rosemary leaves
- Salt and pepper to taste
- 2 tablespoons olive oil

Directions:
1. Heat the griddle pan over medium heat for 5 minutes.
2. Place lamb chops in a bowl and season with garlic powder, rosemary leaves, salt, and pepper.
3. Heat oil and sear the lamb chops—cook for 3 minutes per side.

11. Garlic Butter Lamb Chops

Preparation Time: 5 minutes
Cooking Time: 10 minutes
Servings: 2
Ingredients:
- 1 teaspoon salt
- ½ teaspoon black pepper
- 1 teaspoon minced garlic
- 8 tablespoons butter, at room temperature
- 1 pack French lamb ribs
- ¼ cup herbs of your choice, chopped

Directions:
1. In a bowl, add salt, pepper, garlic, and butter until well combined.
2. Brush all over the lamb.
3. Set the griddle pan on medium-high heat, and then place the lamb on the griddle.
4. Allow to sear and cook for 5 minutes per side.
5. Serve with chopped herbs.

12. Lamb Steak with Caramelized Celeriac

Preparation Time: 5 minutes
Cooking Time: 20 minutes
Servings: 6
Ingredients:

- 2 tablespoons olive oil
- 1 celeriac, peeled and shaved
- 3 pounds lamb steak
- Salt and pepper to taste
- 1 cup chopped mint

Directions:

1. Put olive oil on the griddle pan and sauté the celeriac until caramelized. Set aside.
2. Massage the lamb steak with salt and pepper.
3. Sear the lamb steak on the griddle pan for 3 minutes on each side.
4. Serve with celeriac and chopped mint.

13. Spiced Lamb Burger

Preparation Time: 10 minutes
Cooking Time: 10 minutes
Servings: 4
Ingredients:

- 2 pounds ground lamb
- 1 teaspoon ground coriander
- 1 teaspoon ground cumin
- 2 garlic cloves, minced
- A pinch of cinnamon
- Salt and pepper to taste

Directions:

1. Heat the griddle pan over medium-high heat and brush with olive oil.
2. Place all the ingredients in a bowl and mix to combine.
3. Use your hands to form patties.
4. Cook each side for 5 minutes.

14. Grilled Veal Chops

Preparation Time: 10 minutes
Cooking Time: 10 minutes
Servings: 4
Ingredients:

- 1 tablespoon olive oil
- 2 pounds veal chops
- 4 garlic cloves, minced
- 1 lemon zested
- Salt and pepper to taste
- 1 ½ tablespoon rosemary leaves, chopped

Directions:

1. Heat the griddle pan over medium heat and brush with oil.
2. Place all the ingredients in a bowl and toss to season all sides.
3. Cook on the griddle pan for 5 minutes on each side.
4. Allow resting before slicing.

15. Tuscan-Style Veal Chops

Preparation Time: 10 minutes
Cooking Time: 10 minutes
Servings: 4
Ingredients:

- 2 tablespoons extra-virgin olive oil
- 2 garlic cloves, minced
- 1 tablespoon rosemary leaves, chopped
- ¼ cup sage leaves, chopped
- 4 12-ounce veal ribs
- Salt and pepper to taste

Directions:
1. Heat the griddle pan over medium heat and brush with olive oil.
2. Mix the garlic, rosemary, and sage in a bowl.
3. Rub the herb mixture on the veal and season with salt and pepper to taste.
4. Cook on the griddle pan for 5 minutes on each side.

16. Moose Burger

Preparation Time: 10 minutes
Cooking Time: 10 minutes
Servings: 4
Ingredients:
- 2 pounds ground moose meat
- 2 tablespoons powdered garlic
- 2 tablespoons powdered onion
- 1 teaspoon rosemary, chopped
- Salt and pepper to taste

Directions:
1. Prepare all the ingredients in a bowl. Mix well and form patties using your hands.
2. Heat the griddle pan for 5 minutes and brush the surface with oil.
3. Cook the patties for 5 minutes for each side.
4. Serve on buns.

17. Teriyaki Grilled Venison Medallions

Preparation Time: 6 hours
Cooking Time: 10 minutes
Servings: 4
Ingredients:

- 4 venison tenderloin medallions, sliced to 1-inch thick
- 4 tablespoons soy sauce
- 1 tablespoon honey
- 1 tablespoon toasted sesame oil
- ½ teaspoon rice vinegar
- ¼ teaspoons powdered ginger
- ½ teaspoon powdered garlic
- 1 tablespoon extra-virgin olive oil

Directions:
1. In a mixing bowl, put all the ingredients except the olive oil until well combined.
2. Allow marinating in the fridge for at least 6 hours.
3. Heat the griddle pan over medium heat and brush with olive oil.
4. Sear the venison for 8 minutes.
5. Keep stirring until done.
6. Serve.

18. Venison with Mushrooms

Preparation Time: 10 minutes
Cooking Time: 10 minutes
Servings: 4
Ingredients:
- 1 tablespoon olive oil

- 3 garlic cloves, minced
- 1 onion, chopped
- 4 venison tenderloin medallions, cut into 1-inch thick
- Salt and pepper to taste
- 4 ounces cremini mushrooms, sliced
- 1 teaspoon Dijon mustard
- ½ green onion stalk, minced

Directions:

1. Heat the olive oil on the griddle pan over medium heat.
2. Stir in the garlic and onion and sauté for 2 minutes.
3. Add in the venison and season with salt and pepper to taste.
4. Mix for 3 minutes, and then add the mushrooms.
5. Season with Dijon and cook for another 8 minutes.
6. Garnish with green onions.

19. Lemon Veal Chops

Preparation Time: 10 minutes
Cooking Time: 10 minutes
Servings: 4
Ingredients:

- 4 bone-in rib veal chops
- 6 tablespoons lemon juice, freshly squeezed
- 3 tablespoons minced garlic
- 2 tablespoons lemon zest, grated
- Salt and pepper to taste

Directions:

1. Prepare all the ingredients in a bowl and marinate the veal in the fridge for at least 6 hours.

2. Heat the griddle pan over medium heat and brush with oil.
3. Cook the veal for 5 minutes on each side.

20. Masala Lamb Chops

Preparation Time: 10 minutes
Cooking Time: 10 minutes
Servings: 4
Ingredients:

- 4 lamb chops
- Salt and pepper to taste
- 2 tablespoons curry powder
- 1 teaspoon red pepper flakes
- 1 small red onion, chopped
- 1 large tomato, chopped
- 1 cup Greek yogurt
- 1 tsp Coriander, chopped
- 1 Lemon, sliced

Directions:

1. Heat the griddle pan over high heat. Brush with oil.
2. Season the lamb chops with salt, pepper, curry powder, and red pepper flakes.
3. Sear the lamb chops for 3 to 5 minutes on each side.
4. Meanwhile, mix the red onion, tomatoes, yogurt, and coriander in a bowl. Serve with the yogurt mixture and slices of lemon.

21. Beef Stir Fry

Preparation Time: 1 hour
Cooking Time: 10 minutes
Servings: 4
Ingredients:

- 1 pound steak, sliced

- 4 tablespoons coconut oil
- ½ pound broccoli, cut into florets
- 1 teaspoon fish sauce
- 1 teaspoon sesame oil

For marinade:
- 4 tablespoons coconut aminos
- 2 garlic cloves, chopped
- 1 teaspoon ginger, grated

Directions:
1. Add the sliced meat to a zip-lock bag with garlic, ginger, and coconut aminos and let marinate for 1 hour.
2. Leave the broccoli in boiling water for 2 minutes. Drain well.
3. Drain the marinated meat.
4. Preheat the griddle over high heat.
5. Spray the griddle top with cooking spray.
6. Add the marinated meat onto the hot griddle top and cook for 1–3 minutes or until browned.
7. Add broccoli and stir fry for 3 minutes.
8. Add the fish sauce and sesame oil and stir well.
9. Serve and enjoy.

22. Pork Loin Roast

Preparation Time: 3 hours
Cooking Time: 45 minutes
Servings: 4
Ingredients:
- 1 (3 pounds) pork top loin roast
- Kosher salt to taste
- Black pepper to taste
- Orange marmalade

Directions:
1. Take out any silver skin and excess fat from the loin. Trim the loin to be even in thickness throughout.
2. Coat the loin with kosher salt liberally, place in a resealable bag, and refrigerate for at least 3 hours or overnight. This will dry brine the roast and keep it moist while it cooks.
3. Rinse the excess salt off the roast, pat it dry, and season it with black pepper.
4. Turn the Griddle on high heat and spray it with spray oil.
5. Cook the loin on high heat for several minutes per side until it pulls cleanly from the grill.
6. Get the loin from the griddle and allow it to relax for several minutes to allow the juices to redistribute.
7. Turn the grill down over medium heat and return the loin to the grill. Cook for about 30 minutes, occasionally turning until the internal temperature reaches 145°F. Glaze the outside of the loin with the marmalade, and let it relax for at least 10 minutes before slicing and serving.

23. Healthy Beef & Broccoli

Preparation Time: 10 minutes
Cooking Time: 15 minutes
Servings: 2
Ingredients:
- ½ pound beef, cut into cubes
- ½ cup broccoli florets

- 1 onion, sliced
- 1 tablespoon vinegar
- 1 garlic clove, minced
- 1 tablespoon olive oil
- Salt and pepper to taste

Directions:
1. Preheat the griddle over high heat.
2. Prepare the meat and all the ingredients in a large bowl, toss well, and spread onto the hot griddle top.
3. Cook until the broccoli is tender and the meat is cooked.
4. Serve and enjoy.

24. Steak Kababs

Preparation Time: 10 minutes
Cooking Time: 15 minutes
Servings: 4
Ingredients:
- 1 pound beef sirloin, cut into 1-inch
- 1 green bell pepper, cut into 1-inch
- 1 cup mushrooms
- 1 tablespoon fresh parsley, chopped
- 1 teaspoon garlic, minced
- 2 teaspoons olive oil
- 1 onion, cut into 1-inch pieces
- 3 tablespoons butter
- Salt and pepper to taste

Directions:
1. Preheat the griddle over medium-low heat.
2. Thread the beef, bell pepper, mushrooms, and onion onto the skewers.

3. Brush the meat and vegetables with olive oil and season with pepper and salt.
4. Place skewers onto the hot griddle top and cook for 4–5 minutes per side.
5. Dissolve the butter in a pan over medium-low flame.
6. Add garlic and sauté for a minute.
7. Get the pan from heat and stir in parsley, pepper, and salt.
8. Brush the butter mixture all over kababs. Serve and enjoy.

25. Sticky-sweet Pork Shoulder

Preparation Time: 8 hours
Cooking Time: 20 minutes
Servings: 6–8
Ingredients:
- 1 (5 pounds) Boston Butt pork shoulder

For the Marinade:
- 2 tablespoons garlic, minced
- 1 large piece ginger, peeled and chopped
- 1 cup hoisin sauce
- ¾ cup fish sauce
- 2/3 cup honey
- 2/3 cup Shaoxing
- ½ cup chili oil
- 1/3 cup oyster sauce
- 1/3 cup sesame oil

For the Glaze:
- ¾ cup dark brown sugar
- 1 tablespoon light molasses

Directions:

1. Prepare the meat and all the ingredients in a large bowl, toss well, and spread onto the hot griddle top.
2. Make a shallow cut along the side of the shoulder.
3. Continue cutting deeper into the meat, lifting, and unfurling with your free hand until it lies flat.
4. Purée marinade in a blender and reserve 1 1/2 cups for the glaze, cover, and refrigerate.
5. Pour the remaining marinade in a large sealable plastic bag.
6. Add the pork shoulder to the bag and marinate in the refrigerator for 8 hours.
7. Preheat the griddle over medium heat (with the cover closed, the thermometer should register 350°F).
8. Get the pork from the marinade, letting excess drip off.
9. Add the glaze ingredients to the reserved marinade until sugar is dissolved.
10. Grill the pork for 8 minutes, basting and turning with tongs every minute or so, until thick coated with a glaze, lightly charred in spots, and warmed through; an instant-read thermometer inserted into the thickest part should register 145°F.
11. Move to a cutting board and cut to 1/4 thick to serve.

26. Cuban Pork Chops

Preparation Time: 10 minutes
Cooking Time: 20 minutes
Servings: 4
Ingredients:

- 4 pork chops
- 4 garlic cloves, smashed
- 2 tablespoons olive oil
- 1/3 cup lime juice
- ¼ cup water
- 1 teaspoon ground cumin
- Salt and black pepper

Directions:

1. Set your griddle to medium heat. Salt the pork chops on both sides and cook the chops until lightly browned.
2. Combine the water, garlic, and lime juice in a bowl and whisk until even.
3. Continue cooking the pork chops while basting them with the lime juice mixture.
4. Once the pork chops are cooked, remove the griddle and top with additional sauce and black pepper before serving.

27. Herb Beef Skewers

Preparation Time: 12 hours
Cooking Time: 10 minutes
Servings: 4
Ingredients:

- 2 pounds beef sirloin, cut into cubes
- 2 teaspoons fresh thyme, minced
- 1 tablespoon fresh parsley, minced

- 1 tablespoon lemon zest
- 4 garlic cloves, minced
- 2 tablespoons fresh lemon juice
- ¼ cup olive oil
- 2 teaspoons dried oregano
- 2 teaspoons fresh rosemary, minced
- Salt and pepper to taste

Directions:

1. Add all the ingredients except the meat in a mixing bowl and stir everything well.
2. Add the meat to the bowl and coat well with marinade.
3. Place in the refrigerator for overnight.
4. Preheat the griddle over high heat.
5. Spray the griddle top with cooking spray.
6. Slide the marinated meat onto the skewers.
7. Place the skewers onto the hot griddle top and cook for 6–8 minutes. Turn after every 2 minutes.
8. Serve and enjoy.

28. Glazed Country Ribs

Preparation Time: 15 minutes
Cooking Time: 2 hours
Servings: 6
Ingredients:

- 3 pounds country-style pork ribs
- 1 cup low-sugar ketchup
- ½ cup water
- ¼ cup onion, finely chopped
- ¼ cup cider vinegar
- ¼ cup light molasses

- 2 tablespoons Worcestershire sauce
- 2 teaspoons chili powder
- 2 garlic cloves, minced

Directions:

1. Combine ketchup, water, onion, vinegar, molasses, Worcestershire sauce, chili powder, and garlic in a saucepan and bring to boil.
2. Lower the heat once boiling. Let it simmer for 15 minutes.
3. Trim the fat from the ribs.
4. Preheat the griddle over medium-high heat.
5. Place the ribs, bone-side down, on the griddle, and cook for 1–1/2 to 2 hours or until tender, occasionally brushing with sauce during the last 10 minutes of cooking.
6. Serve with the remaining sauce and enjoy!

29. Cheesy Beef Patties

Preparation Time: 10 minutes
Cooking Time: 12 minutes
Servings: 6
Ingredients:

- 2 pounds ground beef
- 1 teaspoon garlic powder
- 1 cup mozzarella cheese, grated
- 1 teaspoon onion powder
- Salt and pepper to taste

Directions:

1. Prepare all the ingredients into a large bowl and mix until well combined.
2. Preheat the griddle over high heat.

3. Spray the griddle top with cooking spray.
4. Make patties from the meat mixture and place them onto the hot griddle top and cook until golden brown from both sides.
5. Serve and enjoy.

30. Grilled Beef or Calf's Liver

Preparation Time: 10 minutes
Cooking Time: 15 minutes
Servings: 4
Ingredients:

- 1–1 ½ pounds beef or calf's liver
- Salt and pepper to taste
- Lemon wedges for serving

Directions:

1. Prepare all the ingredients.
2. Slice the liver lengthwise into about ½-inch thick slices. Dry the slices with paper towels, then sprinkle with salt and pepper on both sides. Set the knob to the high position. When the griddle is hot, put the liver on the griddle and cook for 8 minutes. Transfer to a platter, rest for 5 minutes, then cut across into slices and serve with lemon wedges.

31. Korean Spicy Pork

Preparation Time: 8 hours
Cooking Time: 10 minutes
Servings: 4
Ingredients:

- 2 pounds pork, cut into 1/8-inch slices

- ½ cup soy sauce
- 5 garlic cloves, minced
- 3 tablespoons minced green onion
- 1 yellow onion, sliced
- 2 tablespoons sesame seeds
- 3 teaspoons black pepper
- ½ cup brown sugar
- 3 tablespoons Gochujang (Korean red chili paste)

Directions:

1. Prepare all the ingredients in a covered glass bowl or resealable bag.
2. Mix well and refrigerate for 8 hours.
3. Heat the griddle grill over high and grill the pork for 2–3 minutes per side until cooked through.
4. Serve immediately on rice or lettuce leaves with soy and kimchi.

32. Greek Lamb Patties

Preparation Time: 15 minutes
Cooking Time: 20 minutes
Servings: 4
Ingredients:

- 1 pound ground lamb
- 5 basil leaves, minced
- 10 mint leaves, minced
- ¼ cup fresh parsley, chopped
- 1 teaspoon dried oregano
- 1 cup feta cheese, crumbled
- 1 tablespoon garlic, minced
- 1 jalapeno pepper, minced
- ¼ teaspoons pepper
- ½ teaspoon kosher salt

Directions:

1. Prepare all the ingredients in a mixing bowl and mix until well combined.
2. Preheat the griddle over high heat.
3. Spray the griddle top with cooking spray.
4. Make four equal shape patties from the meat mixture and place them onto the hot griddle top and cook for 4 minutes on each side.
5. Serve and enjoy.

33. Coffee Crusted Skirt Steak

Preparation Time: 10 minutes
Cooking Time: 20 minutes
Servings: 8
Ingredients:

- ¼ cup coffee beans, finely ground
- ¼ cup dark brown sugar
- 1 ½ teaspoon sea salt
- 1/8 teaspoon ground cinnamon
- Pinch cayenne pepper
- 2 ½ pounds skirt steak
- 1 tablespoon olive oil

Directions:

1. Cut the skirt steak into 4 pieces.
2. Heat the griddle over high.
3. Combine coffee, brown sugar, salt, cinnamon, and cayenne pepper in a bowl to make a rub.
4. Get the steak from the refrigerator and let it rest for 15 minutes.
5. Rub the steak with oil and sprinkle with the spice rub. Massage the spice rub into the meat.
6. Sear until charred and medium-rare, 2 to 4 minutes per side. Place into a cutting board, cover with foil and rest for 5 minutes before thinly slicing against the grain.

34. Pork Cutlet Rolls

Preparation Time: 10 minutes
Cooking Time: 15 minutes
Servings: 4
Ingredients:

- 4 pork cutlets
- 4 sundried tomatoes in oil
- 2 tablespoons parsley, finely chopped
- 1 green onion, finely chopped
- Salt and black pepper to taste
- 2 teaspoons paprika
- ½ tablespoon olive oil
- String for rolled meat

Directions:

1. Prepare all the ingredients.
2. Chop the tomatoes finely, and then add the parsley and green onion. Put salt and pepper.
3. Arrange the cutlets and coat them with the tomato mixture. Roll up the cutlets and secure them intact with the string
4. Massage the rolls with salt, pepper, and paprika powder, and then thinly coat them with olive oil.
5. Bring the griddle grill to high heat. When the griddle is hot, put the cutlet rolls and cook for 15 minutes. Roast until nicely brown and done.
6. Serve with tomato sauce.

35. Grilled Chicken Breast

Preparation Time: 10 minutes
Cooking Time: 12 minutes
Servings: 2
Ingredients:

- 3 tablespoons olive oil
- 5 fresh basil leaves, torn
- 1 garlic clove, sliced
- 2 chicken breasts, boneless, skinless
- Kosher salt and black pepper to taste

Directions:

1. Rub the chicken breasts with black pepper, salt, garlic, basil leaves, and olive oil.
2. Preheat the griddle at 350°F and the upper grill plate on medium heat.
3. Once it is preheated, place the chicken breasts.
4. Cook for 12 minutes. Serve warm.

36. Whiskey Wings

Preparation Time: 10 minutes
Cooking Time: 6 minutes
Servings: 4
Ingredients:

- 1 tablespoon whiskey
- ½ tablespoon chili powder
- 1 teaspoon paprika
- 20 chicken wings
- ¼ teaspoons garlic powder
- Salt and pepper to taste
- 2 teaspoons brown sugar

Directions:

1. Preheat your griddle to 375°F.
2. In the meantime, dump all of the ingredients in a large bowl.
3. With your hands, mix well to coat the chicken wings completely.
4. When the green light is on, arrange the chicken wings onto it.
5. Cook for 6 minutes.
6. Serve with rice and enjoy!

37. Chicken Drumsticks

Preparation Time: 30 minutes
Cooking Time: 40 minutes
Servings: 5
Ingredients:

- 2 tablespoons avocado oil
- 1 tablespoon fresh lime juice
- 1 teaspoon red chili powder
- 1 teaspoon garlic powder
- Salt, as required
- 5 (8-ounce) chicken drumsticks

Directions:

1. In a mixing bowl, mix avocado oil, lime juice, chili powder, salt, and garlic powder and mix well.
2. Add the chicken drumsticks and coat with the marinade generously.
3. Cover the bowl and refrigerate to marinate for about 30–60 minutes.
4. Prepare the griddle to medium-high heat. Place the chicken drumsticks over the grease griddle pan. Cook for about 30–40 minutes, flipping after every 5 minutes. Serve hot.

38. Lemon and Rosemary Turkey and Zucchini Threads

Preparation Time: 10 minutes
Cooking Time: 7 minutes
Servings: 4
Ingredients:

- 1-pound turkey breasts, boneless and skinless
- 1 large zucchini
- 2 tablespoons lemon juice
- ½ teaspoon lemon zest
- ¼ cup olive oil
- 1 tablespoon honey
- 1 tablespoon fresh rosemary
- ¼ teaspoons garlic powder
- Salt and pepper to taste

Directions:

1. Cut the Turkey into smaller chunks and place it inside a bowl.
2. Add the olive oil, lemon juice, zest, honey, rosemary, garlic powder, and salt and pepper to the bowl.
3. With your hands, mix well until the turkey is completely coated with the mixture.
4. Cover and let sit in the fridge for about an hour.
5. Wash the zucchini thoroughly and cut it into small chunks. Season with salt and pepper.
6. Preheat your griddle to 350–375°F.
7. Thread the turkey and zucchini onto soaked (or metal) skewers and arrange them on the plate.
8. Cook for 6–7 minutes. Serve and enjoy!

39. Basil Grilled Chicken with Asparagus

Preparation Time: 10 minutes
Cooking Time: 7 minutes
Servings: 4
Ingredients:

- 1 teaspoon Dijon mustard
- 1 pound chicken breasts, boneless and skinless
- 1 teaspoon dried basil
- 1 teaspoon minced garlic
- 2 tablespoons olive oil
- ¼ teaspoons onion powder
- 12 asparagus spears
- Salt and pepper to taste

Directions:

1. Combine the oil, mustard, basil, garlic, onion powder, and salt and pepper in a bowl.
2. Coat the chicken with this mixture.
3. Meanwhile, preheat your griddle to 350°F.
4. Arrange the chicken breasts onto the plate.
5. Flavor the asparagus with salt and pepper, and then add them next to the chicken.
6. Cook for 7 full minutes, or until your preferred doneness is reached.
7. Serve and enjoy!

40. Thyme Duck Breasts

Preparation Time: 2 hours
Cooking Time: 15 minutes

Servings: 2
Ingredients:

- 2 shallots, sliced thinly
- 1 tablespoon fresh ginger, minced
- 2 tablespoons fresh thyme, chopped
- Salt and ground black pepper, as required
- 2 duck breasts

Directions:

1. In a large bowl, place the shallots, ginger, thyme, salt, and black pepper, and mix well.
2. Add the duck breasts and coat with the marinade evenly.
3. Refrigerate to marinate for about 2 hours.
4. Prepare the griddle pan to high heat.
5. Grease the griddle pan, skin-side down.
6. Place the duck breast over the pan.
7. Cook for about 6–8 minutes per side. Serve hot.

41. Marinated Chicken Kabobs

Preparation Time: 4 hours
Cooking Time: 15 minutes
Servings: 4
Ingredients:

- 1/3 cup extra-virgin olive oil, divided
- 2 garlic cloves, minced
- 1 tablespoon fresh rosemary, minced
- 1 tablespoon fresh oregano, minced
- 1 teaspoon fresh lemon zest, grated
- ½ teaspoon red chili flakes, crushed
- 1-pound chicken breast, boneless and skinless
- 1 ¾ cups green seedless grapes, rinsed
- ½ teaspoon salt
- 1 tablespoon fresh lemon juice

Directions:

1. Cut the chicken breast into 3/4-inch cubes.
2. In a small bowl, add 1/4 cup of oil, garlic, fresh herbs, lemon zest, salt, and chili flakes and beat until well combined.
3. Thread the chicken cubes and grapes onto 12 metal skewers.
4. In a large baking dish, arrange the skewers.
5. Place the marinade and mix well.
6. Refrigerate to marinate for about 4 hours.
7. Prepare the griddle to high heat and grease the pan.
8. Place the chicken skewers over the griddle pan.
9. Cover with the lid and cook for about 3–5 minutes per side or until the chicken is done completely.
10. Remove from the grill and transfer the skewers onto a serving platter.
11. Drizzle with lemon juice and the remaining oil and serve.

42. Teriyaki Chicken Thighs

Preparation Time: 1 hour
Cooking Time: 7 minutes
Servings: 4
Ingredients:

- 4 chicken thighs
- ½ cup brown sugar
- ½ cup teriyaki sauce
- 2 tablespoons rice vinegar
- 1 thumb-sized piece of ginger, minced
- ¼ cup water
- 2 teaspoons minced garlic
- 1 tablespoon cornstarch

Directions:

1. Place the sugar, teriyaki sauce, vinegar, ginger, water, and garlic in a bowl.
2. Mix to combine well.
3. Prepare half of the mixture in a saucepan and set aside.
4. Add the chicken thighs to the bowl and coat well.
5. Cover the bowl with wrap and place in the fridge. Let sit for one hour.
6. Preheat your griddle over medium heat.
7. In the meantime, place the saucepan over medium heat and add the cornstarch. Cook until thickened. Remove from heat and set aside.
8. Arrange the thighs onto the preheated bottom and close the lid.
9. Cook for 5 minutes, then open, brush the thickened sauce over, and cover again.
10. Cook for an additional minute or two. Serve and enjoy!

43. Spiced Chicken Breasts

Preparation Time: 1 hour
Cooking Time: 14 minutes
Servings: 4
Ingredients:

- 2 scallions, chopped
- 1 (1-inch) piece fresh ginger, minced
- 2 garlic cloves, minced
- ¼ cup olive oil
- 2 tablespoons fresh lime juice
- 2 tablespoons low-sodium soy sauce
- 1 teaspoon ground cinnamon
- 1 teaspoon ground cumin
- 1 teaspoon ground turmeric
- Ground black pepper, as required
- 4 (5-ounce) chicken breasts, boneless and skinless

Directions:

1. In a large Ziploc, add all the ingredients and seal it.
2. Mix the bag to coat the chicken with marinade well.
3. Refrigerate to marinate for about 20 minutes to 1 hour.
4. Warm the griddle over high heat and grease the griddle pan.
5. Place the chicken breasts and cook for about 6–7 minutes per side.
6. Serve hot.

44. Maple Glazed Chicken Breasts

Preparation Time: 8 hours
Cooking Time: 15 minutes
Servings: 4
Ingredients:

- ¼ cup extra-virgin olive oil
- 2 tablespoons fresh lemon juice
- 2 tablespoons maple syrup
- 1 garlic clove, minced
- Salt and ground black pepper, as required
- 4 (6-ounce) boneless, skinless chicken breasts

Directions:

1. For the marinade: Get a large bowl, add oil, lemon juice, maple syrup, garlic, salt, and black pepper and beat until well combined.
2. In a large Ziploc, arrange the chicken and marinade.
3. Close and shake to coat well.
4. Refrigerate for 8 hours.
5. Prepare the griddle to medium-high heat, and then grease the griddle pan.
6. Place the chicken and cook for about 5–8 minutes per side.
7. Serve hot.

45. Chili Chicken Skewers

Preparation Time: 10 minutes
Cooking Time: 5 minutes
Servings: 4
Ingredients:

- ¼ cup fresh lime juice
- 2 garlic cloves, sliced
- 1 chipotle chili in adobo, chopped
- Kosher salt and black pepper to taste
- 2 boneless chicken breasts, cut into chunks

Directions:

1. Mix the chicken cubes with black pepper, salt, chili, garlic, and lime juice in a bowl.
2. Thread the chicken cubes on the wooden skewers.
3. Preheat the griddle at 350°F.
4. Once it is warm, place the skewers in the griddle.
5. Grill the skewers for 5 minutes. Serve warm.

46. Paprika Dijon Pork Tenderloin

Preparation Time: 10 minutes
Cooking Time: 20 minutes
Servings: 6
Ingredients:

- 2 1-pound pork tenderloins
- 2 tablespoons Dijon mustard
- 1–½ teaspoons smoked paprika
- 1 teaspoon salt
- 2 tablespoons olive oil

Directions:

1. In a small bowl, put mustard, salt, oil, and paprika, then mix well.
2. Set your griddle to medium heat.
3. Rub the tenderloins with the mustard mixture, making sure they are evenly coated.
4. Place the tenderloins on the griddle and cook until all sides are well browned, and the internal temperature is 135°F.
5. Remove the tenderloins from the griddle and rest for 5 minutes before slicing and serving.

47. Yucatan-Style Grilled Pork

Preparation Time: 4–6 hours
Cooking Time: 10 minutes
Servings: 4
Ingredients:

- 2 pork tenderloins, trimmed
- 1 teaspoon annatto powder
- 1 tablespoon Olive oil

For the Marinade:

- 2 oranges, juiced
- 2 lemons, juiced, or more to taste
- 2 limes, juiced, or more to taste
- 6 garlic cloves, minced
- 1 teaspoon ground cumin
- ½ teaspoon cayenne pepper
- ½ teaspoon dried oregano
- ½ teaspoon black pepper

Directions:

1. Prepare the marinade ingredients in a mixing bowl and whisk until well blended.

2. Cut the tenderloins in half crosswise; cut each piece in half lengthwise.
3. Place the pieces in the marinade and thoroughly coat with the mixture.
4. Cover with plastic wrap and refrigerate for 4 to 6 hours.
5. Transfer the pieces of pork from the marinade to a paper-towel-lined bowl to absorb most of the moisture.
6. Discard paper towels—drizzle olive oil and a bit more annatto powder on the pork.
7. Preheat the griddle over medium-high heat and lightly oil.
8. Place pieces evenly spaced on the griddle; cook for 4 to 5 minutes.
9. Rotate and cook on the other side for another 4 or 5 minutes.
10. Transfer onto a serving platter and allow the meat to rest about 5 minutes before serving.

48. Pineapple Bacon Pork Chops

Preparation Time: 15 minutes
Cooking Time: 40 minutes
Servings: 6
Ingredients:

- 1 large whole pineapple
- 6 pork chops
- 12 slices thick-cut bacon
- 6 Toothpicks, soaked in water

For the Glaze:

- ¼ cup honey
- 1/8 teaspoon cayenne pepper

Directions:

1. Turn both burners to medium-high heat. Turn off one burner after 15 minutes and turn the remaining burners down to medium.
2. Cut and peel the pineapple, cutting the skin off in strips. Slice the pineapple flesh into six quarters.
3. Wrap each pineapple section with a bacon slice; secure each end with a toothpick.
4. Brush the quarters with honey and sprinkle with cayenne pepper.
5. Put the quarters on the griddle, flipping when bacon is cooked so that both sides are evenly grilled.
6. While the pineapple quarters are cooking, coat the pork chops with honey and cayenne pepper. Set on the griddle.
7. Wrap with foil and cook for 20 minutes. Flip, and continue cooking an additional 10 to 20 minutes or until the chops are fully cooked.
8. Serve each chop with a pineapple quarter on the side.

49. Spicy Cajun Pork Chops

Preparation Time: 10 minutes
Cooking Time: 15 minutes
Servings: 4
Ingredients:

- 4 pork chops
- 1 tablespoon paprika
- ½ teaspoon ground cumin
- ½ teaspoon dried sage
- ½ teaspoon salt
- ½ teaspoon black pepper
- ½ teaspoon garlic powder
- ¼ teaspoon cayenne pepper
- 1 tablespoon butter
- 1 tablespoon vegetable oil

Directions:

1. In a mixing bowl, put paprika, cumin, sage, salt, pepper, garlic, and cayenne pepper.
2. Heat your griddle over medium-high heat and add the butter and oil.
3. Rub the pork chops with a generous amount of the seasoning rub.
4. Place the chops on the griddle and cook for 4 to 5 minutes. Turn the pork chops and continue cooking for an additional 4 minutes.
5. Take the pork chops from the griddle and allow to rest for 5 minutes before serving.

50. Honey Soy Pork Chops

Preparation Time: 1 hour
Cooking Time: 15 minutes
Servings: 6
Ingredients:

- 6 (4 ounces) boneless pork chops
- ¼ cup organic honey
- 1 to 2 tablespoons soy sauce, low sodium
- 2 tablespoons olive oil
- 1 tablespoon rice mirin

Directions:

1. Combine honey, soy sauce, oil, and white vinegar and whisk until well combined. Add the sauce and pork chops to a large sealable plastic bag and marinate for 1 hour.
2. Preheat the griddle over medium-high heat and cook for 4 to 5 minutes, or until the pork chop easily releases from the griddle.
3. Flip and continue to cook for 5 additional minutes, or until internal temperature reaches 145°F.
4. Serve and enjoy.

51. Beef Honey Curry Stir Fry

Preparation Time: 15 minutes
Cooking Time: 20 minutes
Servings: 4
Ingredients:

- ½ pound sukiyaki cut beef
- ½ cup honey
- ½ cup soy sauce
- 4 tablespoons curry powder
- 4 tablespoons oil
- 1 teaspoon ground black pepper
- 1 medium-sized red onion, sliced
- 1 medium red bell pepper
- 1 medium green bell pepper
- 1 medium yellow bell pepper

Directions:

1. Cut the red, green, and yellow bell pepper into strips.
2. Mix soy sauce, curry powder, honey, and ground black pepper and marinate the beef for 15 minutes.
3. Prepare your flat top to medium-high heat. Add oil and sauté the red bell pepper, green bell pepper, red onion, and yellow bell pepper for a few minutes, taking care that the vegetables are cooked but not wilted.
4. Take the vegetables off the pan once cooked and set them aside.
5. Remove the beef from the marinade mix and place it on the griddle until halfway cooked. Remove and place in roasting pan.
6. Place the roasting pan on the griddle; add in the remaining half of the oil and marinade.
7. Add the beef and cook on medium heat until the sauce thickens and the beef is cooked through. This only takes 5–7 minutes. Turn off the heat. Toss the cooked vegetables with the beef to coat it with some of the sauce and bring all flavors together. Serve over steaming hot rice, mashed potato, or even pasta.

52. Smoked Pork Sausage Hakka Noodles

Preparation Time: 10 minutes
Cooking Time: 25 minutes
Servings: 4
Ingredients:

- 1 packet Hakka noodles
- 5 smoked pork sausages
- ½ cup coriander leaves

- 1 tablespoon soya sauce
- ½ cup mint leaves
- 1 onion - 3 green chilies
- 1 capsicum - Salt to Taste
- 1 tablespoon Oil
- 1 Cauliflower head

Directions:

1. Cut and slice all the pork vegetables and keep them aside.
2. Then, cook the packet of Hakka noodles in a container. Make sure to add a little bit of oil so that they don't stick together. Boil the noodles for 5–6 minutes.
3. Take the noodles, transfer them to a strainer, and wash them under the tap to stop cooking.
4. Then add a little bit of oil and soya sauce to the noodles. Once this is ready, we are ready to cook the rest of the meal.
5. Prepare the griddle to medium heat. Lightly oil. Add the onions and chilies till they turn light brown.
6. Then add the smoked pork sausages and cook them for 5–7 minutes.
7. Add the coriander and mint leaves and cook for another 5 minutes.
8. Then add the cauliflower, capsicum, and salt to taste.
9. Then add the noodles and then cook them for another 5 minutes.
10. Take it off the griddle and then serve it with mint leaves.

53. Asian Style Beef Broccoli

Preparation Time: 10 minutes
Cooking Time: 10 minutes
Servings: 2
Ingredients:

- ½ pound sukiyaki cut beef, thinly cut
- 3 cups Chinese broccoli
- 1/3 cup water
- 1/3 cup brown sugar
- 1/3 cup soy sauce
- 3 tablespoons cooking oil
- 2 tablespoons browned chopped garlic
- 1–2 tablespoons sesame oil
- ½ teaspoon red chili flakes
- ½ teaspoon freshly ground black pepper

Directions:

1. Get all of your ingredients together.
2. Prepare the griddle to medium heat. Lightly oil. Place the broccoli on the flat top. Cover with basting cover.
3. Put some water to the surface before you cover to steam Chinese broccoli until it is done but not soggy.
4. Cook the beef until browned.
5. Once cooked, put water, soy sauce, brown sugar, half of the garlic, red chili flakes, and black pepper. Let it simmer for 3 minutes.
6. Plate the Chinese broccoli and spoon the cooked beef and its

sauce. Top with the rest of the garlic and sesame oil.

7. Serve and enjoy.

54.   Exotic Asian Pork Burger

Preparation Time: 15 minutes
Cooking Time: 15 minutes
Servings: 4
Ingredients:

- 1 pound ground pork
- 3 tablespoons vinegar (apple cider and white cane vinegar works well)
- 2–3 tablespoons brown sugar
- 1 teaspoon salt
- 1 whole head of garlic (crushed or grated)

Directions:

1. Prepare and mix well all the ingredients.
2. Wait for the pork to get white from the vinegar.
3. Form patties depending on the size and thickness that you want.
4. Prepare your griddle to medium heat. Make smash burgers until thoroughly cooked.
5. Serve over your favorite bun with your choice of condiments and trimmings.
6. As a suggestion, mustard and sriracha provide a great contrast to the tangy and garlicky flavor of the burger. Enjoy!

55.   Oriental Glazed Pork

Preparation Time: 10 minutes
Cooking Time: 10 minutes
Servings: 4
Ingredients:

- 2 pounds pork with the bone left in (best cuts to use are shoulder or pork legs)
- 1-ounce piece of fresh ginger root, sliced thinly
- ½ cup soy sauce
- 1 tablespoon cooking oil
- ½ cup vinegar (cane vinegar or white wine vinegar works well)
- 2/3 cup water
- 1/3 cup brown sugar
- 2–3 pieces star anise

Directions:

1. Wash the pork pieces and place them on the griddle. Prepare the griddle to medium-high heat and sear the pork pieces until some parts are fully browned.
2. Place an aluminum roasting pan on the flat top—over medium heat. Add 1 tablespoon olive oil.
3. Once the pork has been seared, add to the pan although with the ginger slices. Let the ginger infuse with the oil for about a minute.
4. Then add the soy sauce and followed by the water.
5. Put the vinegar. Cover and cook on medium heat until half a cup of the liquid remains.
6. Add sugar and star anise. Dissolve the sugar in the sauce.
7. Glaze pork pieces with the mixture and then cover.
8. Cook for 3 minutes until you can smell the aromatic flavor of the star anise.
9. Serve with plenty of rice.

56. Pot Stickers

Preparation Time: 30 minutes
Cooking Time: 20 minutes
Servings: 6
Ingredients:

- 1-pound lean pork mince
- 1 small head Napa cabbage shredded or cut into slaw-size pieces (about 2 cups)
- 1 teaspoon sesame oil (optional)
- Dumpling wrappers (about 30–36 pieces, exactly 1 packet from the store)
- 1 cup green onion, cut into very small pieces
- 1 teaspoon salt
- Pepper to taste (just a pinch to be on the safe side)
- ½ cup water per cooking batch
- 1 teaspoon oil per cooking batch

Directions:

1. Cook the pork mince halfway through. Remove and let cool.
2. Then in a bowl, combine the pork mince, Napa cabbage, salt, pepper, sesame oil, and green onions.
3. Mix everything together thoroughly until you can make balls out of the mixture and the balls stay formed.
4. Leave the mixture for 30 minutes.
5. When you're ready to make dumplings, place about a tablespoon of the mixture in the center of a dumpling wrapper, wet the edges with a bit of water, and fold over to seal the edges together.
6. To create the dumpling shape, press the dumpling's rounded side down. Repeat until you've gone through all your mixture and dumpling wrappers.
7. To cook, place dumplings on your flat top. Lightly oil the griddle top.
8. Cook covered over medium-high heat. Put some water on the surface before you cover. The steam will cook the dumplings thoroughly.
9. After about 10 minutes, take off the cover. The water will dry up and the dumplings' bottoms will start to fry from the rendered pork fat and the oil.
10. Repeat steps to cook the rest. You can also freeze the uncooked dumplings on a tray until frozen and then transfer them into separate Ziploc bags for 'instant' pan-fried dumplings when you feel like having them.

57. Sweet & Sour Pork Chops with Peppers & Pineapple

Preparation Time: 15 minutes
Cooking Time: 20 minutes
Servings: 4
Ingredients:

- 2 tablespoons extra-virgin olive oil, divided
- 4 boneless pork chops, approximately 1/2" thick
- Sea salt and black pepper to taste
- ¼ cup balsamic vinegar
- ¼ cup real maple syrup
- 3–4 garlic cloves, minced
- 2 teaspoons dried rosemary, chopped
- ½ teaspoon crushed red pepper flakes
- 1 red bell pepper, sliced thin
- 1 yellow bell pepper, sliced thin
- 2 cup fresh pineapple chunks
- 3 large green onions, diced
- ¼ cup fresh parsley, chopped

Directions:

1. Prepare the griddle to medium-high heat. Lightly oil.
2. Put the pork chops and cook for 2 minutes on each side.
3. Flavor with salt and black pepper to taste on each side while cooking.
4. Place an aluminum roasting pan on the flat top. Heat over medium heat.
5. Put vinegar, garlic, maple syrup, rosemary, and red pepper flakes in the pan.
6. Season with salt and black pepper, taste, and occasionally cook, stirring, until slightly thickened, approximately 4–5 minutes.
7. Lower heat and continue to simmer, occasionally stirring, until ready to serve.
8. Meanwhile, add the sliced peppers to the flat top and sear over medium-high heat—season with salt and black pepper to taste. Cook, occasionally stirring, for approximately 8 minutes.
9. Put in the pineapple and continue cooking until heated for approximately 2–3 minutes. Stir in the green onion and parsley and remove from heat.
10. Plate the pork chops, pour the glaze over the pork chops, and serve alongside peppers and pineapple. Enjoy!

CHAPTER 4:

FISH AND SEAFOODS RECIPES

58. Buttered Halibut

Preparation Time: 5 minutes
Cooking Time: 8 minutes
Servings: 2
Ingredients:

- 2 (4-ounce) haddock fillets
- Salt and ground black pepper, as required
- 1 tablespoon butter, melted
- 2 cups lukewarm water

Directions:

1. Flavor the fish fillets with salt and black pepper generously.
2. Place the water tray in the bottom of the griddle.
3. Place about 2 cups of lukewarm water into the water tray.
4. Place the drip pan over the water tray and then arrange the heating element.
5. Now, place the griddle pan over a heating element.
6. Turn on the griddle and set the temperature. Let it preheat over medium heat.
7. After preheating, grease the griddle pan.
8. Place the fish fillets and cover them with the lid. Cook for about 3–4 minutes per side.
9. Remove from the griddle and place the haddock fillets onto serving plates.
10. Drizzle with melted butter and serve.

59. Soy Sauce Salmon

Preparation Time: 5 hours
Cooking Time: 10 minutes
Servings: 4
Ingredients:

- 2 tablespoons scallions, chopped
- ¾ teaspoon fresh ginger, minced
- 1 garlic clove, minced
- ½ teaspoon dried dill weed, crushed
- ¼ cup olive oil
- 2 tablespoons balsamic vinegar
- 2 tablespoons low-sodium soy sauce
- 4 (5-ounce) boneless salmon fillets
- 2 cups lukewarm water

Directions:

1. Add all the ingredients except for the salmon in a large bowl and mix well.

2. Add salmon and coat with marinade generously.
3. Refrigerate to marinate for at least 5 hours.
4. Place the water tray in the bottom of the griddle.
5. Place about 2 cups of lukewarm water into the water tray.
6. Place the drip pan over the water tray and then arrange the heating element.
7. Now, place the griddle pan over a heating element.
8. Plugin the griddle and press the 'Power' button to turn it on.
9. Set the temperature and let it preheat over medium.
10. After preheating, grease the griddle pan. Place the salmon fillets over the griddle pan.
11. Put the lid and cook for 5 minutes per side. Serve hot.

60. Tuna Steak with Avocado & Mango Salsa

Preparation Time: 15 minutes
Cooking Time: 8 minutes
Servings: 2
Ingredients:

- 2 tuna steaks
- 1 ½ tablespoon olive oil
- 1 teaspoon paprika
- 2 tablespoons coconut sugar
- 1 teaspoon onion powder
- ¼ teaspoon pepper
- ½ teaspoon salt
- 2/3 teaspoon cumin

Salsa:

- 1 avocado, pitted and diced
- 1 mango, diced
- 1 tablespoon olive oil
- 1 teaspoon honey
- ½ red onion, diced
- 2 tablespoons lime juice
- Pinch of salt

Directions:

1. Preheat your griddle over medium heat.
2. Place the olive oil and spices in a small bowl and rub the tuna steaks with the mixture.
3. Place on top of the bottom plate and cook for 4 minutes.
4. Flip the steaks over and cook for another 4 minutes.
5. Meanwhile, prepare the salsa by placing all of the salsa ingredients in a bowl and mixing well.
6. Transfer the grilled tuna steaks to two serving plates and divide the avocado and mango salsa among them. Enjoy!

61. Salmon Lime Burgers

Preparation Time: 10 minutes
Cooking Time: 6 minutes
Servings: 2
Ingredients:

- 1 pound skinless salmon fillets, minced
- 2 tablespoons grated lime zest
- 1 tablespoon Dijon mustard
- 3 tablespoons shallot, chopped
- 2 tablespoons fresh cilantro, minced

- 1 tablespoon soy sauce
- 1 tablespoon honey
- 3 garlic cloves, minced
- ½ teaspoon salt
- ¼ teaspoon black pepper

Directions:

1. Thoroughly mix all the ingredients for burgers in a bowl.
2. Make four patties out of this salmon mixture.
3. Preheat the griddle at 350°F and the upper griddle plate on medium heat.
4. Once it is preheated, open the lid and place the salmon burgers in the griddle.
5. Close the griddle's lid and grill the salmon burgers for 6 minutes.
6. Serve warm with buns.

62. Blackened Salmon

Preparation Time: 10 minutes
Cooking Time: 6 minutes
Servings: 2
Ingredients:

- 1 pound salmon fillets
- 3 tablespoons butter, melted
- 1 tablespoon lemon pepper
- 1 teaspoon seasoned salt
- 1 ½ tablespoon smoked paprika
- 1 teaspoon cayenne pepper
- ¾ teaspoon onion salt
- ½ teaspoon dry basil
- ½ teaspoon ground white pepper
- ½ teaspoon ground black pepper
- ¼ teaspoon dry oregano
- ¼ teaspoon ancho chili powder

Directions:

1. Liberally season the salmon fillets with butter and the other ingredients.
2. Preheat the griddle's bottom at 350°F and the upper grill plate on medium heat.
3. Once it is preheated, open the lid and place the salmon fillets in the griddle.
4. Close the griddle's lid and grill the fish fillets for 6 minutes.
5. Serve warm.

63. Lemony Cod

Preparation Time: 5 minutes
Cooking Time: 15 minutes
Servings: 2
Ingredients:

- 1 garlic clove, minced
- ½ tablespoon fresh olive oil
- 1 tablespoon fresh lemon juice
- ½ teaspoon dried rosemary, crushed
- ¼ teaspoon paprika
- Salt and ground black pepper, as required
- 2 (6-ounce) skinless, boneless cod fillets
- 2 cups lukewarm water

Directions:

1. In a mixing bowl, put all the ingredients except the cod fillets.
2. Add the cod fillets and coat with the garlic mixture generously.
3. Place the water tray in the bottom of the griddle.

4. Place about 2 cups of lukewarm water into the water tray.
5. Place the drip pan over the water tray and then arrange the heating element. Now, place the griddle pan over a heating element.
6. Plugin the griddle and press the 'Power' button to turn it on.
7. Set the temperature and let it preheat over medium heat. After preheating, remove the lid and grease the griddle pan.
8. Place the cod fillets over the griddle pan. Put the lid and cook for about 7 minutes per side.
9. Serve hot.

64. Shrimp Kabobs

Preparation Time: 2 hours
Cooking Time: 8 minutes
Servings: 6
Ingredients:
- 1 jalapeño pepper, chopped
- 1 large garlic clove, chopped
- 1 (1-inch) fresh ginger, mined
- 1/3 cup fresh mint leaves
- 1 cup coconut milk
- ¼ cup fresh lime juice
- 1 tablespoon red boat fish sauce
- 24 medium shrimp, peeled and deveined
- 1 avocado, peeled, pitted, and cubed
- 3 cups seedless watermelon, cubed - 2 cups lukewarm water

Directions:
1. In a blender, add jalapeño, garlic, ginger, mint, coconut milk, lime juice, and fish sauce and pulse until smooth.
2. Add the shrimp and coat with the marinade generously.
3. Marinate for at least 2 hours.
4. Remove shrimp from marinade and thread onto pre-soaked wooden skewers with avocado and watermelon.
5. Place the water tray in the bottom of the griddle.
6. Place about 2 cups of lukewarm water into the water tray.
7. Place the drip pan over the water tray and then arrange the heating element.
8. Now, place the griddle pan over a heating element.
9. Plugin the griddle and press the 'Power' button to turn it on.
10. Set the temperature, cover the grill with a lid, and let it preheat over medium heat.
11. After preheating, remove the lid and grease the griddle pan.
12. Place the skewers over the griddle pan.
13. Place the lid and cook for about 3–4 minutes per side.
14. Serve hot.

65. Pesto Shrimp

Preparation Time: 15 minutes
Cooking Time: 10 minutes
Servings: 2
Ingredients:
- 1-pound shrimp, tails, and shells discarded
- ½ cup Pesto Sauce

Directions:

1. Arrange the cleaned shrimp in a bowl and add the pesto sauce to it.
2. Mix gently with your hands until each shrimp is coated with the sauce. Let sit for about 15 minutes.
3. In the meantime, preheat your griddle over medium heat.
4. Open the grill and arrange the shrimp onto the bottom plate.
5. Cook with the lid off for about 2–3 minutes. Rotate and cook for more minutes.
6. Serve as desired and enjoy!

66. Barbecue Squid

Preparation Time: 1 hour
Cooking Time: 3 minutes
Servings: 4
Ingredients:

- 1 ½ pounds skinless squid tubes, sliced
- 1/3 cup red bell pepper, chopped
- 13 fresh red Thai chilies, stemmed
- 6 garlic cloves, minced
- 3 shallots, chopped
- 1 (1-inch) piece fresh ginger, chopped
- 6 tablespoons sugar
- 2 tablespoons soy sauce
- 1 ½ teaspoon black pepper
- ¼ teaspoon salt

Directions:

1. Blend bell pepper, red chilies, shallots, ginger, sugar, soy sauce, black pepper, and salt in a blender.
2. Transfer this marinade to a Ziploc bag and add the squid tubes.

3. Seal the bag and refrigerate for 1 hour for marinate.
4. Preheat the bottom grill of the griddle at 350°F and the upper grill plate on medium heat.
5. Once it is preheated, open the lid and place the squid chunks in the griddle.
6. Close the griddle's lid and grill the squid for 2–3 minutes.
7. Serve warm.

67. Blackened Tilapia

Preparation Time: 10 minutes
Cooking Time: 8 minutes
Servings: 4
Ingredients:

- 4 tilapia fillets
- 3 teaspoons paprika
- ½ teaspoon garlic powder
- ¼ teaspoons onion powder
- ¼ teaspoons black pepper
- ¾ teaspoons salt
- 2 tablespoons olive oil

Directions:

1. Preheat your griddle over medium heat.
2. Place the oil and spices in a small bowl and mix to combine.
3. Rub the mixture into the tilapia fillets, making sure to coat well.
4. When the green light indicates the unit is ready for grilling, arrange the tilapia onto the bottom plate.
5. With the lid off, cook for 4 minutes.
6. Flip over, and then cook for another 4 minutes. Feel free to

increase the cooking time if you like your fish especially burnt.

7. Serve as desired and enjoy!

68. Pistachio Pesto Shrimp

Preparation Time: 30 minutes
Cooking Time: 4 minutes
Servings: 4
Ingredients:

- ¾ cup fresh arugula
- ½ cup fresh parsley, minced
- 1/3 cup shelled pistachios
- 2 tablespoons lemon juice
- 1 garlic clove, peeled
- ¼ teaspoon lemon zest, grated
- ½ cup olive oil
- ¼ cup Parmesan cheese, shredded
- ¼ teaspoon salt
- 1/8 teaspoon pepper
- 1 ½ pounds jumbo shrimp, peeled and deveined

Directions:

1. Start by blending the arugula, parsley, pistachios, lemon juice, garlic, lemon zest, and olive oil in a blender until smooth.
2. Stir in salt, black pepper, Parmesan cheese, and mix well.
3. Toss the shrimp with the prepared sauce in a bowl and then refrigerate for 30 minutes.
4. Thread these pesto shrimps on the wooden skewers.
5. Preheat the bottom grill of the griddle at 350°F and the upper grill plate on medium heat.
6. Once it is preheated, open the lid and place the pesto skewers in the griddle.
7. Close the griddle's lid and grill the shrimp skewers for 4 minutes.
8. Serve warm.

69. Seasoned Tuna

Preparation Time: 5 minutes
Cooking Time: 6 minutes
Servings: 2
Ingredients:

- 2 (6-ounce) yellowfin tuna steaks
- 2 tablespoons blackening seasoning
- Olive oil cooking spray
- 2 cups lukewarm water

Directions:

1. Cover the tuna steaks with the blackening seasoning evenly.
2. Then spray the tuna steaks with cooking spray.
3. Place the water tray in the bottom of the griddle.
4. Place about 2 cups of lukewarm water into the water tray.
5. Place the drip pan over the water tray and then arrange the heating element.
6. Now, place the griddle pan over a heating element.
7. Plugin the griddle and press the 'Power' button to turn it on.
8. Set the temperature and let it preheat over medium heat.
9. After preheating, remove the lid and grease the griddle pan.

10. Place the tuna steaks over the griddle pan.

11. Put the lid and cook for about 2–3 minutes per side. Serve hot.

70. Griddled Salmon with Spring Onion Dressing

Preparation Time: 10 minutes
Cooking Time: 10 minutes
Servings: 4
Ingredients:

- 4 salmon fillets, skin-on
- 2 lemon wedges
- Olive oil, for brushing

For Salsa Dressing

- 1 bunch spring onions,
- 1 large handful parsley leaves, chopped
- ½ red chili, chopped
- 4 tablespoons olive oil
- ½ lemon juice
- 1 tablespoon sherry vinegar

Directions:

1. To prepare the dressing, chop the spring onions without turning them into mush.
2. Combine with parsley and chilies in a mixing bowl.
3. Sprinkle in the oil and mix until all are combined, then add the vinegar and lemon juice. Set aside after seasoning with salt.
4. Prepare the griddle to medium heat.
5. Spray the salmon with some oil and cook on a hot griddle.

6. Cook the salmon fillets for 4 minutes on each side.

7. Serve on a tray with a dish of watercress salad along with lemon wedges.

71. Mahi-Mahi Tacos

Preparation Time: 10 minutes
Cooking Time: 20 minutes
Servings: 4
Ingredients:

- 12 ounces Mahi-Mahi
- 1 tablespoon Vegetable oil
- Lime wedges, for serving
- 2 teaspoons Cajun seasoning
- 1 teaspoon Chili powder
- Kosher salt and pepper to taste
- 12 corn tortillas, street size
- 8 ounces Tartar sauce
- 4 tablespoons Sriracha
- 1 cup lettuce

Directions:

1. Using paper towels, rub the Mahi-Mahi dry and sprinkle both sides with Cajun seasoning, kosher salt, chili powder, and pepper.
2. Preheat the griddle over medium-high heat for 5 minutes. Pour in little oil and cook the fish for 3–4 minutes over it.
3. Flip the fish and brush the opposite side of the grill with additional oil, spreading it evenly before adding the corn tortillas.
4. Cook for another 3 minutes on the fish, then turn the corn tortillas after one minute.

5. After the corn tortillas have crisped to your taste, remove the fish as well as the corn tortillas.

6. Combine the Sriracha and tartar sauce in a mixing bowl. Cut the fish into tiny pieces with a fork.

7. Place the lettuce on the corn tortillas, then top with fish and spicy tartar sauce.

8. Serve with lime wedges on the side.

72. Shrimp Fajitas

Preparation Time: 10 minutes
Cooking Time: 20 minutes
Servings: 4
Ingredients:

- 1 green pepper
- 1 yellow pepper
- 1 red pepper
- 1 tablespoon Avocado oil
- 1 medium yellow onion
- 3 pounds peeled and deveined raw shrimp
- 2 tablespoons Seasoning of Chile Margarita

Directions:

1. Combine the seasoning ingredients and evenly sprinkle over the shrimp and vegetables.

2. Preheat your griddle over medium-high heat and spread some avocado oil on it.

3. Place the vegetables and shrimp onto the griddle and cook for 1–2 minutes, stirring occasionally.

4. Cook till the shrimp is pink and the vegetables are crisp-tender, flipping everything overusing large spatulas.

5. Serve with warm tortillas with your favorite toppings.

73. Lemon Garlic Lobster Tails

Preparation Time: 15 minutes
Cooking Time: 20 minutes
Servings: 4
Ingredients:

- 8 fresh lobster tails
- 4 tablespoons butter, unsalted
- 8 garlic cloves, peeled and grated
- 1 handful parsley leaves
- 1 lemon juice
- Salt and pepper to taste
- Lemon wedges for serving

Directions:

1. Blend the butter, parsley, a pinch of salt, garlic, lemon juice, and pepper in a blender. Process until smooth.

2. If you don't have a blender, soften the butter first, and then stir vigorously with a fork.

3. Preheat a griddle pan at medium-high heat.

4. Cut the lobster tails to half lengthwise. On each tail, add 1/2 tablespoon of butter to the flesh.

5. Put the lobsters on the griddle pan shell side down when it's done.

6. Once the butter melts, it will flavor the lobster meat.

7. Flip the lobster gently, flesh side down, after 2 minutes.

8. Allow around 2–3 minutes for lobster flesh to obtain grill marks and the shell edges to slightly char. Coat the flesh side of the lobster tails with more butter and place them on a serving dish when the meat is opaque.

9. Serve with lemon wedges and some garlic butter, mostly on the side.

74. Blackened Fish Sandwich

Preparation Time: 10 minutes
Cooking Time: 15 minutes
Servings: 6
Ingredients:

- 6 filets of white fish, skinless
- 2 tablespoons blackening seasoning
- 2 tablespoons olive oil
- 6 brioche buns
- Mayo for serving
- Baby arugula for serving

Directions:

1. Massage both sides of the filets with the seasoning and put them aside. Preheat your griddle for 10–15 minutes on medium-low heat. Add some oil to the griddle and set the fish on it. Cook each side for 4–5 minutes.

2. Remove from the griddle and set them aside.

3. Toast the buns, top with the fish, baby arugula, and if wanted, tartar sauce or mayonnaise.

75. Griddled Catfish with Lemon

Preparation Time: 10 minutes
Cooking Time: 15 minutes
Servings: 4
Ingredients:

- 2 catfish fillets
- 1 tablespoon olive oil
- Salt and pepper to taste
- 1 tablespoon butter
- 1 tablespoon lemon juice, freshly squeezed

Directions:

1. In a griddle, melt the oil and butter over medium-high heat.

2. Season the catfish on both sides with pepper and salt before placing it on the griddle. Each side should take about 5–7 minutes.

3. Flip the fish once the first side is done and sprinkle it with lemon juice. Remove from heat once the second side has done cooking and set aside to cool in a few minutes.

76. Buttered Scallops and Shrimp

Preparation Time: 10 minutes
Cooking Time: 20 minutes
Servings: 4
Ingredients:

- 1 pound scallops
- 1 pound shrimp, peeled and deveined - 1 butter pat
- 1 tablespoon lemon pepper

- 1 tablespoon BBQ rub (all-purpose)

Directions:
1. Preheat the griddle over medium-high heat.
2. Using paper towels, pat dry the scallops and shrimp.
3. On the griddle, melt the butter.
4. Put the shrimp in butter and cook for a few minutes.
5. Place the scallops on the griddle and cook until they are light brown.
6. Using the BBQ seasoning, season the scallops.
7. Using the lemon pepper, season the shrimp.
8. Cook for 2 minutes, then rotate the shrimp and scallops.
9. Cook for another 2 minutes. Remove the scallops from the griddle. Check to see if the shrimp has lost its gray color and opaqueness.
10. Cook for an extra minute if the shrimp still is slightly opaque.
11. Serve immediately.

77. Salmon with Honey Soy Glaze

Preparation Time: 10 minutes
Cooking Time: 10 minutes
Servings: 4
Ingredients:
- 4 salmon fillets
- ¼ cup honey
- ¼ cup soy sauce
- 2 limes

- 1 tablespoon Olive oil
- 2 tablespoons Dijon mustard
- 2 tablespoons water
- Pepper and salt to taste
- Asparagus for garnish

Directions:
1. Whisk together soy sauce, honey, lime juice, mustard, and water in a mixing bowl.
2. Preheat your griddle over medium-high temperature.
3. Remove any pin bones you find from salmon fillets.
4. Season the fillets with pepper and salt after coating them with a little oil.
5. Cook the salmon for 3 minutes on each side.
6. Drizzle honey soy glaze over fillets when almost cooked. To evenly reduce the sauce, move it around with your spatula.
7. Garnish with steamed asparagus after removing the fillets and sauce from the heat.

78. King Prawns with a Warm Salad

Preparation Time: 15 minutes
Cooking Time: 20 minutes
Servings: 4
Ingredients:
- 25 king prawns 250g, peeled and defrosted
- 6 crushed garlic cloves
- 1 lemon juice and zest
- 1 teaspoon salt

63 | P a g .

- 3 tablespoons olive oil
- 3 large courgette
- A large bunch asparagus spears
- 100g peas
- A small bunch oregano

Directions:

1. In a mixing bowl, combine the king prawns, lemon zest, garlic, herbed salt, and olive oil. Cover and set aside to chill.
2. Preheat a griddle to 350°F. Spray the courgette ribbons using olive oil, then heat in batches on the griddle until both sides are lightly charred. Leave the peas and asparagus for 2 minutes in boiling water, drain and combine with the oregano and griddled courgette in a salad bowl. Put olive oil and lemon juice into the salad.
3. Thread three marinated prawns into each of the 8 wooden skewers.
4. Cook for 3 minutes on each side of the griddle until done.
5. Serve alongside the salad.

79. Quick Salt & Pepper Squid

Preparation Time: 10 minutes
Cooking Time: 15 minutes
Servings: 4
Ingredients:

- 400g large squid
- 3 tablespoons olive oil
- ½ teaspoon Chinese five-spice
- Sesame oil, to serve
- Coriander sprigs, to serve

- Chili sauce (sweet), to serve
- Salt and black pepper to taste

Directions:

1. Cut the open body of the squid with kitchen scissors and open it out. After a thorough cleaning, pat it dry.
2. Cut the body of a large squid into four roughly square sections.
3. Score its top in a clean crisscross pattern with the blade of a quite sharp knife. Drizzle with oil and lay aside till ready to cook on the griddle.
4. Mix 1 teaspoon of Chinese five-spice, 2 teaspoons of sea salt, and 1 teaspoon of black pepper. Just before cooking, season all sides of the squid with salt and pepper.
5. Heat a griddle pan over high heat and cook for about 1 minute on each side, or until the edges begin to curl.
6. Prepare in a serving dish and a sprinkle of sesame oil. Serve with tiny bowls of chili sauce and coriander leaves to decorate.

80. Tilapia Fish Burgers

Preparation Time: 10 minutes
Cooking Time: 20 minutes
Servings: 4
Ingredients:

- 1 pound tilapia
- ¼ cup panko breadcrumbs
- 1 egg
- 1 egg white
- 2 tablespoons Dijon mustard

- 1 garlic clove, minced
- 1 teaspoon Salt
- 1 teaspoon onion powder
- 1 teaspoon paprika
- ½ teaspoon black pepper
- ½ teaspoon basil
- 1 teaspoon vegetable oil
- 4 hamburger buns
- ½ avocado
- 1 tomato, sliced
- 1 cucumber, sliced

Directions:

1. Process the fish in a food processor until it is finely minced.
2. Combine the fish, breadcrumbs, egg white, mustard, basil, egg, garlic, pepper, salt, paprika, and onion powder in a mixing bowl.
3. Make patties out of the mixture. If necessary, chill the ingredients for 10 minutes before making patties. It will assist them in sticking together.
4. Vegetable oil should be brushed on the burgers.
5. Cook for 4 minutes per side in a medium heated griddle.
6. Serve with avocado, tomato, and cucumber on the toasted buns.

81. Lobster with Garlic-Parsley Butter

Preparation Time: 15 minutes
Cooking Time: 20 minutes
Servings: 4
Ingredients:

- 8 tablespoons butter, unsalted
- 2 tablespoons parsley, finely chopped
- 1 ½ teaspoon red chili flakes, crushed
- 4 garlic cloves, finely chopped
- 1 lemon zest
- salt and black pepper to taste
- 1 ½ pounds lobster
- ¼ cup olive oil

Directions:

1. Set aside a bowl with butter, parsley, chili flakes, salt, garlic, lemon zest, and pepper.
2. Cut the lobster into half lengthwise through the head and tail using a cleaver.
3. Pull off the claws and get out the yellow-green tomalley. Place the lobster halves on a baking sheet, shell side down, crack claws, and then place them upon on baking sheet.
4. Season the claws and halves with salt and pepper after drizzling with oil.

5. Set a griddle to high heat. Put lobster halves, flesh sides down, claws on the hottest portion of the griddle; cook for 2–3 minutes, or until slightly charred.

6. Turn the lobster over and brush it with garlic-parsley butter with a spoon.

7. Continue cooking until the lobster meat is cooked, about 3 minutes more.

82. Seared Sea Scallops with Capers and Brown Butter

Preparation Time: 25 minutes
Cooking Time: 20 minutes
Servings: 4
Ingredients:

- 1 ½ pounds sea scallops
- 2 tablespoons olive oil
- 5 tablespoons brown butter
- 3 tablespoons capers
- 2 tablespoons parsley - Salt to taste

Directions:

1. Colossal scallops should be rinsed in cold water and dried with paper towels.

2. Place the scallops on a cookie sheet lined with paper towels, then top with another layer of paper towels. Refrigerate for 20–25 minutes after placing the tray in the refrigerator.

3. Set the griddle to high direct heat. Allow 10–15 minutes for the griddle pan to heat up over the heat source.

4. Remove the scallops from the refrigerator and brush each side with olive oil before seasoning with just a pinch of salt.

5. Place the scallops in melted brown butter on a heated griddle surface and sear each side for 2 minutes. Serve with capers and parsley.

83. Flavorful Mexican Shrimp

Preparation Time: 10 minutes
Cooking Time: 13 minutes
Servings: 4
Ingredients:

- 1 pound shrimp, cleaned
- 3 tablespoons fresh parsley, chopped
- 1 tablespoon garlic, minced
- ¼ onion, sliced
- ¼ teaspoons paprika
- ¼ teaspoons ground cumin
- 2 fresh lime juice
- 2 tablespoons olive oil
- ¼ cup butter
- Salt and pepper to taste

Directions:

1. Season the shrimp with paprika, cumin, pepper, and salt.

2. Preheat the griddle over high heat.

3. Add oil and butter to the griddle top. Sauté onion and garlic for 5 minutes.

4. Add the shrimp and cook for 5–8 minutes or until cooked.

5. Add parsley and lime juice.

6. Stir well and serve.

84. Coconut Pineapple Shrimp Skewers

Preparation Time: 1 hour
Cooking Time: 5 minutes
Servings: 4
Ingredients:

- 1–½ pounds uncooked jumbo shrimp
- ½ cup light coconut milk
- 1 tablespoon cilantro, chopped
- 4 teaspoons Tabasco Original Red Sauce
- 2 teaspoons soy sauce
- ¼ cup freshly squeezed orange juice
- ¼ cup squeezed lime juice
- 3/4-pound pineapple, cut into 1-inch chunks
- Olive oil for grilling

Directions:

1. Peel and deveined the jumbo shrimp.
2. Combine the coconut milk, cilantro, Tabasco sauce, soy sauce, orange juice, lime juice. Add the shrimp and toss to coat.
3. Refrigerate to marinate for 1 hour.
4. Thread the shrimp and pineapple onto metal skewers, alternating each.
5. Preheat the griddle over medium heat and add oil.
6. Cook 5 minutes, flipping once, until the shrimp turn opaque pink.
7. Serve immediately.

85. Crab-stuffed Trout

Preparation Time: 10 minutes
Cooking Time: 15 minutes
Servings: 4
Ingredients:

- 12 ounces crabmeat, picked over for shells and cartilage
- 1 cup chopped seeded fresh tomato, drained if necessary
- Grated zest of 1 lemon
- 1 tablespoon olive oil + more for brushing the fish
- 2 scallions, trimmed and chopped
- Salt and pepper to taste
- 4 8- to 10-ounce rainbow trout, cleaned and butterflied
- Lemon wedges for serving

Directions:

1. Put the crab, tomato, and lemon zest in a medium bowl. Put the oil and scallions in a small skillet over medium heat; cook, occasionally stirring, until softened, 2 to 3 minutes.
2. Add to the crab, sprinkle with salt and pepper, toss gently, taste, and adjust the seasoning.
3. Pat the trout dry with paper towels. Put oil and sprinkle with salt and pepper on both sides.
4. Divide the crab mixture between the trout, filling their cavities. Pull the two sides closed, pushing the filling in, if needed, to keep it from spilling out.
5. Bring the griddle grill to high heat, oil the griddle, and allow it to heat.

Put the trout with the open side of the fish facing you and cook until the skin browns and the fish release easily, 8 to 10 minutes.

6. Carefully turn the fish, using a second spatula to lower them back down to the grates.

7. Close the lid and cook until the stuffing is heated through, 4 to 5 minutes.

8. Transfer the trout to a platter and serve with lemon wedges.

86. Pop-open Clams with Horseradish-tabasco Sauce

Preparation Time: 10 minutes
Cooking Time: 10 minutes
Servings: 4
Ingredients:

- 2 dozen littleneck clams, scrubbed
- 4 tablespoons unsalted butter, softened
- 2 tablespoons horseradish, drained
- 1 tablespoon hot sauce, like Tabasco
- ¼ teaspoon lemon zest, finely grated
- 1 tablespoon fresh lemon juice
- ¼ teaspoon smoked paprika
- Sea salt to taste

Directions:

1. Preheat the griddle over high.
2. Blend the butter with the horseradish, hot sauce, lemon zest, lemon juice, paprika, and a pinch of salt.

3. Arrange the clams over high heat and grill until they pop open, about 25 seconds.

4. Carefully turn the clams overusing tongs so the meat side is down.

5. Grill for about 20 seconds longer until the clam juices start to simmer.

6. Transfer the clams to a serving bowl.

7. Put 1/2 teaspoon of the sauce and serve.

87. Bacon-Wrapped Scallops

Preparation Time: 5 minutes
Cooking Time: 5 minutes
Servings: 4
Ingredients:

- 12 large sea scallops, side muscle removed
- 8 slices bacon
- 1 tablespoon vegetable oil
- 12 toothpicks

Directions:

1. Warm the griddle over medium heat, add oil, and cook the bacon until the fat has been rendered, but the bacon is still flexible.

2. Remove the bacon from the griddle and place it on paper towels.

3. Raise the griddle heat to medium-high.

4. Wrap each scallop with a half slice of bacon and skewer with a toothpick to keep the bacon in place.

5. Place the scallops on the griddle and cook for 90 seconds per side.

They should be lightly browned on both sides.

6. Remove from the griddle and serve immediately.

88. Italian Shrimp

Preparation Time: 5 minutes
Cooking Time: 5 minutes
Servings: 4
Ingredients:
- 1 pound shrimp, deveined
- 1 teaspoon Italian seasoning
- 1 teaspoon paprika
- 1 ½ teaspoon garlic, minced
- 1 stick butter - 1 fresh lemon juice
- ¼ teaspoons pepper
- ½ teaspoon salt

Directions:
1. Preheat the griddle over high heat.
2. Melt butter on the hot griddle top.
3. Add garlic and cook for 30 seconds. Toss the shrimp with paprika, Italian seasoning, pepper, and salt. Add the shrimp into the pan and cook for 2–3 minutes per side.
4. Drizzle lemon juice over shrimp.
5. Stir and serve.

89. Halibut Fillets with Spinach and Olives

Preparation Time: 10 minutes
Cooking Time: 10 minutes
Servings: 4
Ingredients:
- 4 (6 ounces) halibut fillets
- 1/3 cup olive oil
- 4 cups baby spinach
- ¼ cup lemon juice
- 2 ounces pitted black olives, halved
- 2 tablespoons flat-leaf parsley, chopped
- 2 teaspoons fresh dill, chopped
- Lemon wedges, to serve

Directions:
1. Preheat the griddle over medium heat.
2. Toss the spinach with lemon juice in a mixing bowl and set aside.
3. Brush the fish with olive oil and cook for 3–4 minutes per side, or until cooked through.
4. Remove from heat, cover with foil, and let rest for 5 minutes.
5. Add the remaining oil and cook the spinach for 2 minutes, or until just wilted. Remove from heat.
6. Toss with olives and herbs, transfer to serving plates with fish, and serve with lemon wedges.

90. Spicy Grilled Squid

Preparation Time: 10 minutes
Cooking Time: 5 minutes
Servings: 4
Ingredients:
- 1 ½ pounds squid, prepared
- 1 tablespoon Olive oil

For the Marinade:
- 2 garlic cloves, minced
- ½ teaspoon ginger, minced
- 3 tablespoons gochujang
- 3 tablespoons corn syrup
- 1 teaspoon yellow mustard
- 1 teaspoon soy sauce
- 2 teaspoons sesame oil

69 | P a g .

- 1 teaspoon sesame seeds
- 2 green onions, chopped

Directions:

1. Preheat the griddle over medium-high heat and brush with olive oil.
2. Add the squid and tentacles to the griddle and cook for 1 minute until the bottom looks firm and opaque.
3. Turn them over and cook for another minute; straighten out the body with tongs if it curls.
4. Baste with sauce on top of the squid and cook for 2 additional minutes. Flip and baste the other side, cook for 1 minute until the sauce evaporates and the squid turns red and shiny.

91. Grilled Popcorn Shrimp

Preparation Time: 10 minutes
Cooking Time: 3 minutes
Servings: 5
Ingredients:
Spice Rub:

- 2 teaspoons garlic powder
- 2 teaspoons sweet paprika
- 1 teaspoon onion powder
- 1 teaspoon dried oregano
- 1 teaspoon cayenne pepper
- 1 teaspoon salt
- 1 teaspoon freshly ground black pepper
- 1 teaspoon sugar

Shrimp:

- 1 ½ pound shelled and deveined small shrimp
- 1 lemon, cut into wedges

Directions:

1. In a Ziploc, mix well the spices and shake to blend them.
2. Add the shrimp to the plastic bag with the spice rub and shake to coat.
3. Turn the control knob to the high position. Oil the griddle and allow it to heat until the oil is shimmering but not smoking.
4. Grill the shrimp for 1 minute each side until they are opaque and firm to the touch.
5. Serve the shrimp immediately in a bowl garnished with lemon wedges (and with plenty of napkins).

92. Shrimp Veggie Stir Fry

Preparation Time: 10 minutes
Cooking Time: 10 minutes
Servings: 2
Ingredients:

- ½ pound shrimp, peeled and deveined
- 1 tablespoon garlic, minced
- 1/3 cup olives
- 1 cup mushrooms, sliced
- 2 tablespoons olive oil
- 1 cup tomatoes, diced
- 1 small onion, chopped
- ¼ pepper
- ¼ salt

Directions:
1. Preheat the griddle over high heat. Add oil.
2. Add the onion, mushrooms, and garlic and sauté until the onion is soft.
3. Add the shrimp and tomatoes and stir until the shrimp is cooked through. Add olives and stir well.
4. Remove the pan from heat and set aside for 5 minutes—season with pepper and salt.
5. Serve and enjoy.

93. Spiced Crab Legs

Preparation Time: 5 minutes
Cooking Time: 5 minutes
Servings: 4
Ingredients:
- 4 pounds king crab legs, cooked
- 2 tablespoons chili oil
- Butter for serving

Directions:
1. Preheat the griddle over high heat.
2. Brush both sides of the crab legs with chili oil and place them on the grill. Tent with foil.
3. Cook for 4 to 5 minutes, turning once. Transfer to plates and serve with drawn butter.

94. Sardines with Lemon and Thyme

Preparation Time: 5 minutes
Cooking Time: 8 minutes
Servings: 2
Ingredients:
- 1-pound fresh sardines, cleaned
- ½ olive oil for brushing the fish
- ¼ salt and pepper
- 1 small bunch of fresh thyme
- Lemon wedges for serving

Directions:
1. Put oil on the fish and season with salt and pepper on both sides and in the cavity. Tuck in the thyme sprigs.
2. Bring the griddle grill to high heat. Oil the griddle and allow it to heat. Put the fish and cook until the skin is charred in places and the fish release easily, 8 minutes.
3. Prepare the fish to a platter and serve with lemon wedges and a final sprinkle of salt.

95. Lump Crab Cakes

Preparation Time: 10 minutes
Cooking Time: 10 minutes
Servings: 4
Ingredients:
- 1 pound lump crab meat
- ½ cup panko breadcrumbs
- 1/3 cup mayonnaise
- 1 egg, beaten
- 2 tablespoons Dijon mustard
- 2 teaspoons Worcestershire sauce
- ½ teaspoon paprika
- ½ teaspoon salt
- ¼ teaspoon black pepper
- 3 tablespoons vegetable oil

Directions:
1. Preheat the griddle over medium heat.

2. In a large bowl, prepare crab, breadcrumbs, mayo, egg, mustard, Worcestershire sauce, paprika, salt, and pepper. Mix well to combine.

3. Form the crab mixture into 4 large balls and flatten them slightly.

4. Add the oil to the griddle and cook the crab cakes for approximately 5 minutes per side or until browned and crispy. Serve immediately.

96. Caper Basil Halibut

Preparation Time: 5 minutes
Cooking Time: 8 minutes
Servings: 4
Ingredients:

- 24 ounces halibut fillets
- 2 garlic cloves, crushed
- 2 tablespoons olive oil
- 2 teaspoons capers, drained
- 3 tablespoons fresh basil, sliced
- 2 ½ tablespoons fresh lemon juice
- Salt and pepper to taste

Directions:

1. In a bowl, blend together garlic, olive oil, capers, and lemon juice. Stir in 2 tablespoons of basil.

2. Season the garlic mixture with pepper and salt.

3. Season fish fillets with pepper and salt and brush with the garlic mixture. Preheat the griddle over high heat. Place the fish fillets on a hot griddle and cook for 4 minutes on each side.

4. Transfer the fish fillets to a serving plate and top with the remaining garlic mixture and basil.

5. Serve and enjoy.

97. Honey-lime Tilapia

Preparation Time: 10 minutes
Cooking Time: 15 minutes
Servings: 4
Ingredients:

- 4 fillets tilapia
- 2 tablespoons honey
- 4 limes, thinly sliced
- 2 ears corn, shucked
- 2 tablespoons fresh cilantro leaves
- ¼ cup olive oil
- ¼ kosher salt
- ¼ ground black pepper

Directions:

1. Preheat the griddle over high heat.
2. Cut 4 squares of foil about 12 inches long.
3. Put the piece of tilapia in each foil. Add honey, and then top with lime, corn, and cilantro.
4. Put olive oil and flavor with sea salt and pepper. Cook until the tilapia is cooked through and the corn is tender, about 15 minutes.

98. Garlic Butter Tilapia

Preparation Time: 10 minutes
Cooking Time: 8 minutes
Servings: 6
Ingredients:

- 2 pounds tilapia fillets
- 1 teaspoon garlic powder
- ½ fresh lemon juice

- 1 tablespoon butter, melted
- Salt and pepper to taste

Directions:

1. In a bowl, put lemon juice, garlic powder, and butter and microwave for 10 seconds.
2. Brush both sides of the fish fillet with the lemon mixture. Season the fillet with pepper and salt.
3. Preheat the griddle over high heat.
4. Spray griddle top with cooking spray.
5. Place the fillets on a hot griddle top and cook for 4 minutes on each side.
6. Serve and enjoy.

99. Swordfish Skewers

Preparation Time: 10 minutes
Cooking Time: 10 minutes
Servings: 4
Ingredients:

- 1 ½ pounds skinless swordfish fillet
- 2 teaspoons lemon zest
- 3 tablespoons lemon juice
- ½ cup finely chopped parsley
- 2 teaspoons garlic, minced
- ¾ teaspoon sea salt
- ¼ teaspoon black pepper
- 2 tablespoons extra-virgin olive oil, plus extra for serving
- ½ teaspoon red pepper flakes
- 3 lemons, cut into slices

Directions:

1. Preheat the griddle over medium-high heat.

2. Combine lemon zest, parsley, garlic, 1/4 teaspoon of salt, and pepper in a small bowl with a fork to make gremolata and set aside.
3. Mix the swordfish pieces with the reserved lemon juice, olive oil, red pepper flakes, and the remaining salt. Thread the swordfish and lemon slices, alternating each, onto the metal skewers.
4. Grill the skewers for 10 minutes, rotating halfway through, or until the fish is cooked through.
5. Prepare the skewers on a serving platter and sprinkle them with gremolata.
6. Drizzle with olive oil and serve.

100. Greek Salmon Fillets

Preparation Time: 10 minutes
Cooking Time: 6 minutes
Servings: 2
Ingredients:

- 2 salmon fillets
- 1 tablespoon fresh basil, minced
- 1 tablespoon butter, melted
- 1 tablespoon fresh lemon juice
- 1/8 teaspoons salt

Directions:

1. Preheat the griddle over high heat.
2. In a bowl, place lemon juice, basil, butter, and salt.
3. Brush the salmon fillets with the lemon mixture and place them on the hot griddle top. Cook the salmon for 2–3 minutes. Flip the salmon and cook for 2–3 minutes more. Serve and enjoy.

101. Butterflied Shrimp with Spicy Miso Glaze

Preparation Time: 10 minutes
Cooking Time: 15 minutes
Servings: 4
Ingredients:

- ½ cup any miso
- ¼ cup mirin (alternative: 2 tablespoons. each honey and water mixed)
- 1 tablespoon sriracha or other garlicky hot sauce
- Salt and pepper (optional)
- 2 pounds jumbo or colossal shrimp (21/25 or under 15 count), peeled
- 3 tablespoons chopped scallion greens

Directions:

1. Beat the miso, sriracha, and mirin in a bowl until smooth. Taste and adjust according to your taste.
2. Butterfly the shrimp—layout butterfly shrimp out in a single layer on a rimmed baking sheet.
3. Glaze the shrimp, then turn them all over and brush the other side.
4. Bring the griddle grill to high heat. Oil the griddle.
5. Put the shrimp on the griddle grill, flattening them quickly by hand or with tongs as you work.
6. Cook until the shrimp are not transparent, and the glaze is browned, 7 to 8 minutes per side, depending on their size. Garnish with the scallion greens and serve.

102. Tuna with Fresh Tomato-basil Sauce

Preparation Time: 10 minutes
Cooking Time: 25 minutes
Servings: 4
Ingredients:
Tomato-Basil Sauce:

- 2 tablespoons olive oil
- 1 small yellow onion, diced
- ¼ teaspoon salt
- ½-pint cherry tomatoes
- 2 tablespoons water
- ¼ cup fresh basil leaves, chopped

Tuna:

- 1 tablespoon olive oil
- 4 tuna steaks (1 inch thick)

Directions:

1. Cut the cherry tomatoes in half.
2. In a griddle pan, warm olive oil over medium heat. Add the onion and salt.
3. Cook, frequently stirring, until the onion is golden brown, 10 to 15 minutes. Add the tomatoes and water and cook for approximately 5 to 7 minutes, until the tomatoes have softened and wrinkled. Stir in the basil just before serving.
4. Bring the griddle grill to high heat. Oil the griddle. Rub the olive oil over the tuna steaks. Grill for about 4 minutes. To test for doneness, prod on the edge of the tuna with a fork.

5. The fish should flake, but the center will still be a bit rosy. Spoon the tuna into 4 shallow bowls and top with the warm tomato-basil sauce.

103. Scallops with Lemony Salsa Verde

Preparation Time: 15 minutes
Cooking Time: 5 minutes
Servings: 2
Ingredients:

- 1 tablespoon olive oil (add more for grilling)
- 12 large sea scallops, side muscle removed
- Sea salt for seasoning

For the Lemony Salsa Verde:

- ½ lemon, with peel, seeded, and chopped
- 5 tomatillos, peeled and pulsed in a blender
- 1 small shallot, finely chopped
- 1 garlic clove, finely chopped
- ¼ cup olive oil
- ¾ cup finely chopped fresh parsley
- ½ cup finely chopped fresh cilantro
- ¼ cup chopped fresh chives
- ¼ teaspoon sea salt
- ¼ teaspoon black pepper

Directions:

1. Toss the Lemony Salsa ingredients in a small mixing bowl and set aside.
2. Preheat the griddle over medium-high and brush with olive oil.

3. Toss the scallops with 1 tablespoon olive oil on a baking sheet and season with salt.
4. Add the scallops to the griddle, turning once after 45 seconds to 1 minute.
5. Cook an additional 1 minute before removing from the griddle.
6. Serve the scallops topped with the Lemony Salsa Verde.

104. Seafood Stuffed Sole

Preparation Time: 15 minutes
Cooking Time: 15 minutes
Servings: 2
Ingredients:

- ¼ cup shrimp, cooked, peeled, and chopped
- 1 tablespoon lemon juice
- 2 tablespoons butter, melted, divided
- ¾ cup cherry tomatoes
- 1 tablespoon chicken broth
- ½ can (6-ounces) crabmeat, drained
- ½ teaspoon parsley, fresh minced
- 1 tablespoon whipped cream cheese
- ½ teaspoon grated lemon zest
- 2 tablespoons breadcrumbs
- 1 teaspoon chive, minced
- 2 (6-ounces) sole fish fillets, cut from the side with gutted and cleaned
- ¼ teaspoon black ground pepper
- Salt to taste

Directions:

1. Mix your cream cheese, crabmeat, shrimp, garlic, lemon zest, parsley, 2 tablespoons of butter, breadcrumbs, and chive in a mixing bowl.
2. Stuff each fillet with 1/4 of this mixture and secure the ends with toothpicks.
3. Mix lemon juice, tomatoes, salt, and pepper in a different bowl.
4. Place your stuffed fillets in a foil sheet and top with the tomato mixture.
5. Cover and seal the fillets in foil.
6. Preheat your griddle grill in a medium-temperature setting.
7. Once your grill is preheated, place 2 sealed fillets on the grill.
8. Grill it for 7 minutes per side. Serve and enjoy!

105. Grilled Oysters with Spiced Tequila Butter

Preparation Time: 10 minutes
Cooking Time: 10 minutes
Servings: 6
Ingredients:

- 3 dozen medium oysters, scrubbed and shucked
- Flakey sea salt, for serving

For the Butter

- ¼ teaspoon crushed red pepper
- 7 tablespoons unsalted butter
- ¼ teaspoon chili oil
- 1 teaspoon dried oregano
- 2 tablespoons freshly squeezed lemon juice
- 2 tablespoons tequila Blanco

Directions:

1. Combine the butter ingredients in a small mixing bowl until well incorporated and set aside.
2. Preheat the griddle over high heat.
3. Grill the oysters for about 2 minutes.
4. Sprinkle the oysters with salt flakes.
5. Warm the butter in a microwave for 30 seconds and spoon the warm tequila butter over the oysters and serve.

106. Parmesan Shrimp

Preparation Time: 20 minutes
Cooking Time: 5 minutes
Servings: 4
Ingredients:

- 1 pound shrimp, peeled and deveined
- 2 tablespoons Parmesan cheese, grated
- 1 tablespoon fresh lemon juice
- 1 tablespoon pine nuts, toasted
- 1 garlic clove
- ½ cup basil
- 1 tablespoon olive oil
- Salt and pepper to taste

Directions:

1. Add basil, lemon juice, cheese, pine nuts, garlic, pepper, and salt in a blender and blend until smooth.
2. Add the shrimp and basil paste to a bowl and mix well.
3. Place the shrimp bowl in the fridge for 20 minutes.

4. Preheat the griddle over high heat.

5. Spray the griddle top with cooking spray.

6. Thread the marinated shrimp onto skewers and place the skewers on the hot griddle top.

7. Cook the shrimp, each side for 3 minutes or until cooked.

8. Serve and enjoy.

107. Mussels with Pancetta

Preparation Time: 10 minutes
Cooking Time: 15 minutes
Servings: 4
Ingredients:

- ¾ cup mayonnaise
- 1 tablespoon minced garlic
- 1 4-ounce slice pancetta, chopped
- Salt and pepper to taste
- 4 pounds mussels
- 8 thick slices of Italian bread
- ¼ cup good-quality olive oil

Directions:

1. Whisk the mayonnaise and garlic together in a small bowl.

2. Put the pancetta in a small cold skillet and turn the heat to low; cook, occasionally stirring, until the meat turns golden and crisp and most of the fat is rendered, about 5 minutes.

3. Pat on a paper towel, then stir into the mayonnaise along with 1 teaspoon of the rendered fat from the pan. Taste and add more garlic and some salt and pepper if you like.

4. Cover and refrigerate until you're ready to serve. (You can make the aioli up to several days ahead; refrigerate in an airtight container.)

4. Clean the mussels and pull off any beards. Discard any that are broken or don't close when tapped.

5. Put oil on both sides of the bread slices.

6. Bring the griddle grill to high heat. Oil the griddle. Toast the bread, turning once, until it develops grill marks with some charring, 1 to 2 minutes per side. Remove from the grill and keep warm.

7. Scatter the mussels onto the griddle, spreading them out so they are in a single layer—Cook for 3 minutes.

8. Prepare the open mussels in a large bowl with tongs. If any have not opened, leave them on the grill, cook for another minute or 2, check frequently, and the remove open mussels until they are all off the grill.

9. Dollop the aioli over the tops of the mussels and use a large spoon to turn the mussels over to coat them.

10. Serve the mussels drizzled with their juices, either over or alongside the bread.

108. Crisp-skin Salmon with Maple-ginger Glaze

Preparation Time: 10 minutes
Cooking Time: 10 minutes

Servings: 6

Ingredients:

- 1 2-pound skin-on salmon fillet
- 1 tablespoon good-quality vegetable oil
- Salt and pepper to taste
- ¼ cup maple syrup
- 1 tablespoon Dijon mustard
- 1 tablespoon minced fresh ginger

Directions:

1. Remove the remaining pin bones from the salmon. Score the skin in a crosshatch pattern.
2. Dry the fish with paper towels and put it on a baking sheet. Add oil on the skin side, flavor with salt and pepper on both sides.
3. Add maple syrup, mustard, and ginger in a bowl and stir to combine. Brush the glaze over the top.
4. Bring the griddle grill to high heat. When the griddle is hot, put the salmon skin side down and cook, without turning, for 10 minutes; check with a sharp knife and peek inside to check a couple of times.
5. Transfer the salmon to a cutting board, cut into 4 or 6 pieces, and serve.

109. Beer Whitefish with Mayo

Preparation Time: 5 minutes
Cooking Time: 10 minutes
Servings: 4
Ingredients:
For the Roasted Garlic Mayo:

- 3 egg yolks, at room temperature
- 1 tablespoon squeezed lemon (alternative- lime juice)
- 1 ¾ cups oil - 2 tablespoons roasted garlic
- 2 teaspoons salt

For the Beer-Battered Fish:

- 5 cups oil, plus more as needed
- 1 ½ cups all-purpose flour (add more for coating)
- 1 teaspoon ancho chili powder
- 1 teaspoon salt, plus more for seasoning
- ½ teaspoon baking soda
- 1 (12-ounce/340-g) can dark beer
- 2 pounds (907 g) boneless, skinless white fish fillets, such as cod or amberjack, cut into 1 ½-inch-thick strips

Directions:

1. To make the mayo: Combine the egg yolks and lemon juice in a blender or food processor.
2. Blend for 30 seconds, and while continuing to blend, slowly drizzle in the oil; the mixture should become thick and emulsified.
3. Add the garlic and salt and blend just to combine. The mayo can be stored, covered in the refrigerator for up to 3 days.
4. To prepare the fish: Preheat the griddle over medium-high heat and brush with olive oil.
5. Combine the flour, chili powder, salt, and baking soda in a large bowl. While whisking, add the beer slowly and continue whisking until

smooth; it should have the consistency of pancake batter.

6. Season the fish fillets with salt, coat with plain flour, and dip into the beer batter. Let some batter drip back into the bowl and gently lay the fish in the oil (work in batches and don't let the fish pieces touch).

7. Cook for 3 minutes (use a metal spatula or slotted spoon to flip) until deep golden brown and crisp. Take with a spoon and drain on a wire rack or a plate lined with paper towels. Serve with garlic mayo.

110. Cilantro Fish with Lime

Preparation Time: 5 minutes
Cooking Time: 8 minutes
Servings: 4
Ingredients:

- 4 cups oil, plus more as needed
- 4 garlic cloves
- 1 white onion, quartered
- 1 jalapeño chili, stemmed, halved, and seeded
- 1 (3- to 5-pound/1.4- to 2.3-kg) whole fish, such as snapper, striped bass, or hogfish, scaled and gutted
- Salt, for seasoning
- 1 bunch cilantro (leaves only)
- Juice of 2 limes (about 1/4 cup)

Directions:

1. Preheat the griddle over medium-high heat and brush with olive oil. Add the garlic, onion, and jalapeño and cook until the garlic is cooked through but not burnt, about 3 minutes. Use tongs to remove the garlic and set it aside.

2. Using a sharp knife, cut 2 or 3 deep slits into both sides of the fish, careful not to cut through the bone.

3. Push the onion and jalapeño to the sides of the griddle and add the fish.

4. Cook until golden brown and crisp. Then rotate the fish with a spatula and cook for another 5 minutes, or just until cooked through (cut into it; the flesh should be opaque and flake with a fork).

5. Keep stirring the onion and jalapeño as well; they should be tender and browned by the time the fish is cooked.

6. Remove the fish with two slotted spoons and drain on a wire rack or a plate lined with paper towels— season with salt.

7. Scoop the garlic, onion, and jalapeño into a food processor or mortar and pestle and add the cilantro and lime juice.

8. Blend until smooth, flavor with salt, and serve warm with the fish.

111. Trout with Cumin and Burnt Citrus Vinaigrette

Preparation Time: 7 minutes
Cooking Time: 15 minutes
Servings: 4
Ingredients:

- 1 ½ tablespoon cumin seeds
- 3 oranges
- 3 lemons
- 1 ½ cups oil, plus more for coating
- 3 tablespoons honey, plus more for coating
- ¼ cup vinegar
- ½ shallot, grated
- 1 ½ teaspoons salt
- ½ teaspoon Mexican oregano
- 4 whole rainbow trout, 12 to 16 ounces (340 to 454 g) each, scaled and gutted
- Oil and salt, for coating

Directions:

1. Preheat the griddle over medium-high heat and brush with olive oil.
2. To make the vinaigrette: Add the cumin to the griddle and shake over medium heat until toasted and fragrant, about 2 minutes. Grind until very fine in a spice grinder or blender and set aside.
3. Zest 1 orange and 1 lemon and set the zest aside. Slice all oranges and lemons in half, then toss in about 1 tablespoon each of oil and honey, just enough to coat.
4. Place the citrus cut side down on the griddle over medium heat and grill until nicely charred and fragrant, 1 to 2 minutes once they have cooled, juice to get about 1 1/2 cups of juice.
5. Combine the juice, vinegar, shallot, orange and lemon zest, cumin, salt, oregano, and the

remaining 2 tablespoons of honey in a bowl.
6. Beat until salt and honey have dissolved. While whisking, slowly pour in the 11/2 cups of oil and continue to whisk until emulsified.
7. To cook the trout: Open and gently press each fish, so it lies flat. Rub the fish with oil and salt.
8. Place skin side down over medium heat and cook until the skin is browned and crisp, and the flesh turns opaque, 4 to 5 minutes.
9. Serve the fish folded back over (so it looks again like a whole fish).

112. Lime Snapper Ceviche

Preparation Time: 20 minutes
Cooking Time: 25 minutes
Servings: 4
Ingredients:
For the Marinade:

- 1 cucumber
- 1 cup squeezed lime juice
- 1 jalapeño chili, stemmed
- ½ cup basil leaves
- 1 teaspoon salt

For the Pickled Onions:

- 8 spring onions, white and green parts (may substitute large scallions)
- Oil, for coating
- 1 teaspoon salt, plus more for coating
- 1 teaspoon sugar
- Vinegar, for pickling

For the Grilled Cucumber

- 1 cucumber

- Oil and salt, for coating
- 1 ½ pound (680 g) boneless, skinless snapper or any other whitefish
- Salt, for seasoning
- ½ cup basil leaves, coarsely chopped
- 1 celery stalk, thinly sliced

Directions:

1. Preheat the griddle over medium-high heat and brush with olive oil.

2. To make the marinade: In a blender, combine the cucumber with the lime juice, jalapeño, basil, and salt and blend until smooth.

3. Transfer to a fine-mesh strainer or cheesecloth over a large bowl and push the mixture through with a rubber spatula, discard solids. Set the bowl over ice to cool.

4. To prepare the onions: Cut the green tops from the onions. Toss the greens in oil and salt and cook over high heat for about 1 minute, just until charred, then chop coarsely and set aside.

5. Slice the white parts of the onions as thinly as possible and place in a bowl with 1 teaspoon of salt, sugar, and enough vinegar to cover. Set aside to pickle while prepping the remaining ingredients.

6. To prepare the cucumber: Cut the cucumber lengthwise and remove the seeds.

7. Toss with oil and salt and grill over medium heat just until charred, 1 to 2 minutes per side. Cut into roughly matchstick-size strips about 1 inch long.

8. With your sharpest knife, slice the fish at a 45-degree angle into very thin (about 1/8 inch) slices, then cut crosswise into pieces approximately 2 inches long. (Freezing the fish for about 20 minutes before slicing can make it easier to slice evenly.)

9. When you are ready to serve, salt the fish lightly. Add the marinade and mix well.

10. Stir in the drained pickled onions, grilled onion greens, cucumber, chopped basil, and celery.

11. Serve immediately.

113. Tuna Steaks with Ginger

Preparation Time: 30 minutes
Cooking Time: 15 minutes
Servings: 4
Ingredients:

- 2 tablespoons salt
- 2 teaspoons cayenne pepper
- 2 teaspoons sweet paprika
- 1 teaspoon ground white pepper
- 1 teaspoon celery salt
- 1 tablespoon fresh ginger, peeled and grated
- 1 large garlic clove, grated
- 2 tablespoons oil
- 1 tablespoon honey
- 2 (12-ounce/340-g) tuna steaks, about 1 1/2 inches thick
- Oil for drizzling
- Lemon wedges, for serving

Directions:

1. To make the rub: Mix the salt, cayenne, paprika, white pepper, celery salt, ginger, garlic, oil, and honey in a small bowl.
2. Cover the tuna with the wet rub, massage for about 3 minutes, then refrigerate uncovered for 30 to 60 minutes.
3. Preheat the griddle over medium-high heat and brush with olive oil.
4. When you are ready to cook, place the tuna steaks on the griddle, with at least 2 inches between them.
5. Using a thin metal fish spatula, flip the tuna after 2 minutes, careful not to let the fish flake apart. Cook for another 2 minutes.
6. Place to a cutting board and let the fish rest for 4 to 5 minutes. Slice the tuna along (not against) the grain.
7. Serve, drizzle it with oil and serve it with the lemon wedges.

114. Spinach Halibut with Olives

Preparation Time: 10 minutes
Cooking Time: 10 minutes
Servings: 4
Ingredients:

- 4 (6-ounce/170-g) halibut fillets
- 1/3 cup olive oil
- 4 cups baby spinach
- ¼ cup lemon juice
- 2 ounces (57 g) pitted black olives, halved
- 2 tablespoons flat-leaf parsley, chopped
- 2 teaspoons fresh dill, chopped
- Lemon wedges, to serve

Directions:

1. Preheat the griddle over medium heat.
2. Toss the spinach with lemon juice in a mixing bowl and set aside.
3. Brush the fish with olive oil and cook for 3–4 minutes per side, or until cooked through.
4. Get from heat, cover with foil, and let rest for 5 minutes.
5. Add the remaining oil and cook the spinach for 2 minutes, or until just wilted. Remove from heat.

6. Toss with olives and herbs, transfer to serving plates with fish, and serve with lemon wedges.

115. Spiced Snapper with Salsa

Preparation Time: 10 minutes
Cooking Time: 20 minutes
Servings: 4
Ingredients:

- 2 red snappers, cleaned
- Sea salt, to taste
- 1/3 cup tandoori spice
- Olive oil, plus more for the grill
- Extra-virgin olive oil for drizzling
- Lime wedges, for serving

For the Salsa:

- 1 ripe but firm mango, peeled and chopped
- 1 small red onion, thinly sliced
- 1 bunch cilantro, coarsely chopped
- 3 tablespoons fresh lime juice

Directions:

1. Put mango, onion, cilantro, lime juice, and a big pinch of salt in a medium mixing bowl; add some olive oil and toss again to coat.
2. Place the snapper on a cutting board and pat dry with paper towels. Cut slashes crosswise on a diagonal along the body every 2 inches on both sides. Cut all the way down to the bones.
3. Season the fish generously inside and out with salt—coat the fish with tandoori spice.
4. Preheat the griddle medium-high heat and brush with oil.
5. Grill the fish for 10 minutes, undisturbed, until the skin is puffed and charred.
6. Flip and grill the fish until the other side is lightly charred and skin is puffed for 8 to 12 minutes.
7. Transfer to a platter.
8. Top with mango salad and serve with lime wedges.

CHAPTER 5:

VEGETABLE RECIPES

116. Spinach and Cheese Portobello

Preparation Time: 5 minutes
Cooking Time: 5 minutes
Servings: 3
Ingredients:

- 3 Portobello mushrooms
- 2 cups spinach, chopped
- 1 cup shredded cheddar cheese
- 4 ounces cream cheese
- 1 tablespoon olive oil
- 1 teaspoon minced garlic
- Salt and pepper, to taste

Directions:

1. Preheat your grill to 350°F.
2. Clean the mushroom caps well and pat dry with paper towels.
3. Remove the stems so that the filling can fit.
4. Now, make the filling by mixing the cheeses, spinach, garlic, salt, and pepper. Divide this mixture among the mushrooms.
5. Drizzle with olive oil.
6. When the green light is on, open the grill and add the mushrooms.

7. Arrange on top of the plate and cook with the lid off for about 5 minutes.
8. Now, lower the lid gently, but do not use pressure. Let cook for 15–20 seconds, just so the cheese melts faster.
9. Transfer to a serving plate and enjoy!

117. Caprese Eggplant Boats

Preparation Time: 10 minutes
Cooking Time: 10 minutes
Servings: 4
Ingredients:

- 2 eggplants
- 1 cup cherry tomatoes, halved
- 1 cup mozzarella balls, chopped
- 2 tablespoons olive oil
- 4 tablespoons chopped basil leaves
- Salt and pepper, to taste

Directions:

1. Preheat your grill to 375°F.
2. Cut the eggplants in half (no need to peel them, just wash well), put olive oil, then flavor with salt and pepper generously.
3. When the green light is on, open the grill and arrange the eggplant halves onto the bottom plate.

4. Lower the lid and cook for about 4–5 minutes, until well done.
5. Transfer to a serving plate and top with cherry tomatoes, mozzarella, and basil.
6. Serve and enjoy!

118. Grilled Tofu with Pineapple

Preparation Time: 10 minutes
Cooking Time: 8 minutes
Servings: 4
Ingredients:
- 1-pound firm tofu
- 1 red bell pepper
- 1 yellow bell pepper
- 1 zucchini
- ½ pineapple
- ½ teaspoon ginger paste
- Salt and pepper, to taste
- 2 tablespoons olive oil

Directions:
1. Preheat your grill over medium-high heat.
2. Meanwhile, chop the tofu and veggies into smaller chunks, and place them in a bowl. If using wooden skewers, soak them into the water before using.
3. Add ginger and oil to the bowl and mix until coated well.
4. Arrange the veggies and tofu onto the skewers.
5. When the green light turns on, open the grill, and arrange the skewers onto the bottom plate.
6. Cook for 4 minutes, then rotate and cook for additional 4 minutes.

7. Serve as desired and enjoy!

119. Garlic Mixed Veggies

Preparation Time: 10 minutes
Cooking Time: 10 minutes
Servings: 4
Ingredients:
- 1 bunch fresh asparagus, trimmed
- 6 ounces fresh mushrooms, halved
- 6 Campari tomatoes, halved
- 1 red onion, cut into 1-inch chunks
- 3 garlic cloves, minced
- 2 tablespoons olive oil
- Salt and ground black pepper, as required
- 2 cups lukewarm water

Directions:
1. In a big bowl, prepare all the ingredients and toss to coat well.
2. Place the water tray in the bottom of the griddle.
3. Place about 2 cups of lukewarm water into the water tray.
4. Place the drip pan over the water tray and then arrange the heating element.
5. Now, place the griddle pan over a heating element.
6. Plugin the griddle and press the 'Power' button to turn it on.
7. Set the temperature and let it preheat over medium heat.
8. After preheating, grease the griddle pan.
9. Place the vegetables over the griddle pan.

10. Put the lid and cook for about 8 minutes, flipping occasionally.

120. Guacamole

Preparation Time: 1 hour
Cooking Time: 5 minutes
Servings: 4
Ingredients:

- 2 ripe avocados, halved and pitted
- 2 teaspoons vegetable oil
- 3 tablespoons fresh lime juice
- 1 garlic clove, crushed
- ¼ teaspoon ground chipotle chili
- Salt, as required
- ¼ cup red onion, chopped finely
- ¼ cup fresh cilantro, chopped finely
- 2 cups lukewarm water

Directions:

1. Brush the cut sides of each avocado half with oil.
2. Place the water tray in the bottom of the griddle.
3. Place about 2 cups of lukewarm water into the water tray.
4. Place the drip pan over the water tray and then arrange the heating element.
5. Now, place the griddle pan over a heating element.
6. Set the temperature and let it preheat over medium.
7. After preheating, grease the griddle pan.
8. Place the avocado halves over the griddle pan, cut side down.

9. Cook uncovered for about 2–4 minutes.
10. Transfer the avocados onto the cutting board and let them cool slightly.
11. Remove the peel and transfer the flesh into a bowl.
12. Add the lime juice, garlic, chipotle, and salt, and with a fork, mash until almost smooth.
13. Stir in onion and cilantro and refrigerate, covered for about 1 hour before serving.

121. Pineapple & Veggie Skewers

Preparation Time: 10 minutes
Cooking Time: 15 minutes
Servings: 6
Ingredients:

- 1/3 cup olive oil
- 1 ½ teaspoon dried basil
- ¾ teaspoon dried oregano
- Salt and ground black pepper, as required
- 2 zucchinis, cut into 1-inch slices
- 2 yellow squash, cut into 1-inch slices
- ½-pound whole fresh mushrooms
- 1 red bell pepper, cut into chunks
- 1 red onion, cut into chunks
- 12 cherry tomatoes
- 1 fresh pineapple, cut into chunks
- 2 cups lukewarm water

Directions:

1. In a bowl, add oil, herbs, salt, and black pepper and mix well.

2. Thread the veggies and pineapple onto pre-soaked wooden skewers.
3. Brush the veggies and pineapple with the oil mixture evenly.
4. Place the water tray in the bottom of the griddle.
5. Place about 2 cups of lukewarm water into the water tray.
6. Place the drip pan over the water tray and then arrange the heating element.
7. Now, place the griddle pan over a heating element.
8. Plugin the griddle and press the 'Power' button to turn it on.
9. Set the temperature and let it preheat over medium.
10. After preheating, grease the griddle pan.
11. Place the skewers over the griddle pan.
12. Put the lid and cook for about 10–15 minutes, flipping occasionally.
13. Serve hot.

122. Haloumi Kebabs

Preparation Time: 10 minutes
Cooking Time: 5 minutes
Servings: 4
Ingredients:

- ½-pound Haloumi cheese
- 4 cremini mushrooms, cut in half
- 1 zucchini, cut into chunks
- ½ bell pepper, cut into chunks
- 2 tablespoons olive oil
- Salt and pepper, to taste

Directions:

1. Preheat your griddle to 375°F.

2. Meanwhile, leave 8 wooden skewers in water to prevent burning.
3. Cut the cheese into chunks.
4. Thread the cheese and veggies onto the skewers, drizzle with the olive oil and sprinkle with salt and pepper.
5. Arrange onto the bottom plate, lower the lid, and cook closed for about 5 minutes (or more if you want it well done).
6. Serve as desired and enjoy!

123. Goat Cheese & Tomato Stuffed Zucchini

Preparation Time: 5 minutes
Cooking Time: 8 minutes
Servings: 8
Ingredients:

- 14 ounces goat cheese
- 1 ½ cups tomato sauce
- 4 medium zucchinis

Directions:

1. Preheat your grill over medium-high heat.
2. Slice the zucchini in half and scoop the seeds out.
3. Coat the grill with cooking spray and add the zucchini to it.
4. Lower the lid and cook for 2 minutes.
5. Now, add half of the goat cheese first, top with tomato sauce, and place the remaining cheese on top.
6. Arrange a piece of aluminum foil on top of the filling to make a big mess.

7. Carefully lower the grill and cook for an additional minute.
8. Serve and enjoy!

124. Paprika & Chipotle Lime Cauli-steaks

Preparation Time: 10 minutes
Cooking Time: 6 minutes
Servings: 4
Ingredients:

- 2 cauliflower heads
- 4 tablespoons olive oil
- 1 teaspoon minced garlic
- 1 tablespoon chipotle powder
- 1 ½ tablespoons paprika
- 1 teaspoon honey
- 1 teaspoon salt
- Juice of 1 large lime
- 1 teaspoon lime zest

Directions:

1. Preheat your grill over medium-high heat.
2. Get the outer leaves of the cauliflower and trim them well. Lay them flat onto your cutting board and then cut them into steak-like pieces (about 3 to 4 inches thick).
3. In a bowl, beat all of the remaining ingredients.
4. Brush the steaks with the mixture well, and then arrange them onto the bottom plate of the grill.
5. Lower the lid to cut the cooking time in half, and cook only for about 6 minutes, without turning over.

6. Transfer to a serving plate and enjoy!

125. Stuffed Zucchini

Preparation Time: 15 minutes
Cooking Time: 25 minutes
Servings: 6
Ingredients:

- 3 medium zucchinis, sliced in half lengthwise
- 1 teaspoon vegetable oil
- Salt and ground black pepper, as required
- 3 cup corn, cut off the cob
- 1 cup Parmesan cheese, shredded
- 2/3 cup sour cream
- ¼ teaspoon hot sauce
- Olive oil cooking spray
- 2 cups lukewarm water

Directions:

1. Slice the ends off the zucchini and cut in half lengthwise.
2. Scoop out the pulp from each half of zucchini, leaving the shell.
3. For filling: in a large pan of boiling water, add the corn over medium heat and cook for about 5–7 minutes. Drain and set it aside to cool.
4. In a large bowl, add corn, half of the Parmesan cheese, sour cream, oil, salt, pepper, and hot sauce, and mix well.
5. Spray the zucchini shells with cooking spray evenly.
6. Place the water tray in the bottom of the griddle.

7. Place about 2 cups of lukewarm water into the water tray.

8. Place the drip pan over the water tray and then arrange the heating element.

9. Now, place the griddle pan over a heating element.

10. Plugin the griddle and press the 'Power' button to turn it on.

11. Set the temperature and let it preheat over medium.

12. After preheating, remove the lid and grease the griddle pan.

13. Place the zucchini halves over the griddle pan, flesh side down.

14. Place the lid and cook for about 8–10 minutes.

15. Remove the zucchini halves from the grill. Spoon filling into each zucchini half evenly and sprinkle with the remaining Parmesan cheese. Place the zucchini halves over the griddle pan. Put the lid and cook for about 8 minutes.

16. Serve hot.

126. Mediterranean Veggies

Preparation Time: 1 hour
Cooking Time: 10 minutes
Servings: 4
Ingredients:

- 1 cup mixed bell peppers, chopped
- 1 cup eggplant, chopped
- 1 cup zucchini, chopped
- 1 cup mushrooms, chopped
- ½ cup onion, chopped
- ½ cup sun-dried tomato vinaigrette dressing

- 2 cups lukewarm water

Directions:

1. Prepare all the ingredients in a mixing bowl and toss to coat well.

2. Refrigerate to marinate for about 1 hour. Place the water tray in the bottom of the griddle.

3. Place about 2 cups of lukewarm water into the water tray.

4. Place the drip pan over the water tray and then arrange the heating element.

5. Now, place the griddle pan over a heating element.

6. Plugin the griddle and press the 'Power' button to turn it on.

7. Set the temperature, cover the grill with a lid and let it preheat over medium.

8. After preheating, remove the lid and grease the griddle pan.

9. Place the vegetables over the griddle pan. Put the lid and cook for 8–10 minutes, flipping occasionally. Serve hot.

127. Grilled Basil Pizza

Preparation Time: 10 minutes
Cooking Time: 5 minutes
Servings: 1
Ingredients:

- 1 tortilla
- 3 tablespoons tomato sauce
- 3 ounces shredded mozzarella cheese
- 4 basil leaves, chopped
- Pinch of salt

Directions:

1. Preheat your griddle over medium-high heat.
2. Unlock to lower the griddle and lay it on your counter.
3. When the green light turns on, add the tortilla to the griddle and lower the lid.
4. Cook only for about 40 seconds, just until it becomes hot.
5. Add the tomato sauce on top, sprinkle with cheese, basil, and some salt.
6. Cook for another minute or so—with the lid off—until the cheese becomes melted.
7. Serve and enjoy!

128. Stir Fry Mushrooms

Preparation Time: 10 minutes
Cooking Time: 10 minutes
Servings: 2
Ingredients:

- 10 ounces mushrooms, sliced
- ¼ cup olive oil
- 1 tablespoon garlic, minced
- ¼ teaspoons dried thyme
- Salt and pepper to taste

Directions:

1. Preheat the griddle over high heat.
2. Add some oil to the hot griddle top.
3. Add mushrooms, garlic, thyme, pepper, and salt and sauté until tender.
4. Drizzle the remaining oil and serve.

129. Stir Fry Vegetables

Preparation Time: 10 minutes
Cooking Time: 20 minutes
Servings: 4
Ingredients:

- 2 medium potatoes
- 3 medium carrots
- ¼ cup olive oil
- 1 small rutabaga
- 2 medium parsnips
- ¼ pepper
- ¼ salt

Directions:

1. Preheat the griddle over high heat.
2. Cut and peel the potatoes, carrots, rutabaga, and parsnips into small pieces.
3. In a mixing bowl, toss the vegetables with olive oil, salt, and pepper.
4. Transfer the vegetables onto the hot griddle top and stir fry until the vegetables are tender.
5. Serve and enjoy.

130. Healthy Zucchini Noodles

Preparation Time: 10 minutes
Cooking Time: 15 minutes
Servings: 4
Ingredients:

- 4 small zucchinis, spiralized
- 1 tablespoon soy sauce
- 2 onions, spiralized
- 2 tablespoons olive oil
- 1 tablespoon sesame seeds
- 2 tablespoons teriyaki sauce

Directions:

1. Preheat the griddle over high heat.
2. Add oil to the hot griddle top.

3. Add onion and sauté for 4–5 minutes.

4. Put the zucchini noodles and cook for 2 minutes.

5. Add sesame seeds, teriyaki sauce, and soy sauce and cook for 4–5 minutes.

6. Serve and enjoy.

131. Easy Seared Green Beans

Preparation Time: 10 minutes
Cooking Time: 10 minutes
Servings: 6
Ingredients:

- 1 ½ pounds green beans, trimmed
- 1 ½ tablespoons rice vinegar
- 3 tablespoons soy sauce
- 1 ½ tablespoon sesame oil
- 2 tablespoons sesame seeds, toasted
- 1 ½ tablespoons brown sugar
- ¼ teaspoon black pepper

Directions:

1. Prepare boiling water and cook the green beans for 3 minutes, then drain well.

2. Transfer the green beans to chilled ice water and drain again—Pat dry the green beans.

3. Preheat the griddle over high heat.

4. Add oil to the hot griddle top.

5. Add green beans and stir fry for 2 minutes.

6. Add soy sauce, brown sugar, vinegar, and pepper and stir fry for 2 minutes more.

7. Add sesame seeds and toss well to coat. Serve and enjoy.

132. Stir Fry Bok Choy

Preparation Time: 10 minutes
Cooking Time: 5 minutes
Servings: 4
Ingredients:

- 2 heads bok choy, trimmed and cut crosswise
- 1 teaspoon sesame oil
- 2 teaspoons soy sauce
- 2 tablespoons water
- 1 tablespoon butter
- 1 tablespoon peanut oil
- 1 tablespoon oyster sauce
- ½ teaspoon salt

Directions:

1. Prepare a small bowl, put together soy sauce, oyster sauce, sesame oil, water, and set aside.

2. Preheat the griddle over high heat.

3. Add oil to the hot griddle top.

4. Place the bok choy and salt and stir fry for 2 minutes. Add butter and the soy sauce mixture and stir fry for 1–2 minutes.

5. Serve and enjoy.

133. Stir Fry Cabbage

Preparation Time: 10 minutes
Cooking Time: 5 minutes
Servings: 4
Ingredients:

- 1 cabbage head, tear cabbage leaves, washed and drained
- 2 green onion, sliced
- 1 tablespoon ginger, minced
- 2 garlic cloves, minced
- 1 tablespoon soy sauce

- ½ tablespoon vinegar
- 4 dried chilies
- 2 tablespoons olive oil
- ½ teaspoon salt

Directions:

1. Preheat the griddle over high heat.
2. Add oil to the hot griddle top.
3. Add ginger, garlic, and green onion and sauté for 2–3 minutes.
4. Add dried chilies and sauté for 30 seconds.
5. Add cabbage, vinegar, soy sauce, and salt and stir fry for 1–2 minutes over high heat until the cabbage is wilted.
6. Serve and enjoy.

134. Pineapple Fried Rice

Preparation Time: 10 minutes
Cooking Time: 10 minutes
Servings: 4
Ingredients:

- 3 cups cooked brown rice
- ½ cup frozen corn
- 2 carrots, peeled and grated
- 1 onion, diced
- 2 garlic cloves, minced
- 2 tablespoons olive oil
- ½ teaspoon ginger powder
- 1 tablespoon sesame oil
- 3 tablespoons soy sauce
- ¼ cup green onion, sliced
- 2 cups pineapple, diced
- ½ cup frozen peas

Directions:

1. In a small bowl, mix well the soy sauce, ginger powder, and sesame oil and set aside.

2. Preheat the griddle over high heat.
3. Add oil to the hot griddle top.
4. Add onion and garlic and sauté for 3–4 minutes.
5. Add corn, carrots, and peas and constantly stir for 3–4 minutes.
6. Stir in the cooked rice, green onions, pineapple, and the soy sauce mixture and stir continuously for 2–3 minutes.
7. Serve and enjoy.

135. Italian Zucchini Slices

Preparation Time: 10 minutes
Cooking Time: 5 minutes
Servings: 4
Ingredients:

- 2 zucchinis, cut into 1/2-inch-thick slices
- 1 teaspoon Italian seasoning
- 2 garlic cloves, minced
- ¼ cup butter, melted
- 1 ½ tablespoon fresh parsley, chopped
- 1 tablespoon fresh lemon juice
- Salt and pepper to taste

Directions:

1. Prepare a bowl, add the melted butter, lemon juice, Italian seasoning, garlic, pepper, and salt.
2. Brush the zucchini slices with the melted butter mixture.
3. Preheat the griddle over high heat.
4. Place the zucchini slices on the griddle top and cook for 2 minutes per side.

5. Transfer the zucchini slices to a serving plate and garnish with parsley.
6. Serve and enjoy.

136. Honey Vegetables

Preparation Time: 10 minutes
Cooking Time: 5 minutes
Servings: 4
Ingredients:

- 2 medium zucchinis, cut into matchsticks
- 2 tablespoons coconut oil
- 2 teaspoons garlic, minced
- 1 tablespoon honey
- 3 tablespoons soy sauce
- 1 teaspoon sesame seeds
- 2 cups carrots, cut into matchsticks
- 2 cups snow peas

Directions:

1. Get a small bowl, put soy sauce, garlic, and honey, and set aside.
2. Preheat the griddle over high heat.
3. Add oil to the hot griddle top.
4. Add carrots, snow peas, and zucchini, and sauté for 1–2 minutes.
5. Add the soy sauce mixture and stir fry for 1 minute.
6. Garnish with sesame seeds and serve.

137. Green Onion Rice

Preparation Time: 10 minutes
Cooking Time: 10 minutes
Servings: 2
Ingredients:

- 4 cups rice, cooked
- 2 large eggs
- 2 tablespoons green onion, sliced
- 2 tablespoons olive oil
- 1 teaspoon salt

Directions:

1. In a bowl, whisk eggs and set aside.
2. Preheat the griddle over high heat.
3. Spray the griddle top with cooking spray.
4. Add the cooked rice to the hot griddle top and fry until the rice separates from each other.
5. Push the rice to one side of the griddle top. Add oil to the griddle and pour a beaten egg.
6. Add salt and mix egg quickly with rice and cook until the rice grains are covered by egg.
7. Put the green onion and stir fry for 2 minutes. Serve and enjoy.

138. Polenta with Rosemary

Preparation Time: 5 minutes
Cooking Time: 10 minutes
Servings: 3
Ingredients:

- 24-ounce log prepared polenta
- 2 teaspoon extra-virgin olive oil
- Garlic salt to taste
- Lemon pepper to taste
- 2 tablespoons chopped rosemary

Directions:

1. Preheat the griddle on high heat. Cut the polenta into 12 1/2-inch thick slices. Place the slices on a baking sheet.

2. Put oil on both sides of the polenta rounds and season lightly with garlic salt, lemon pepper, and sprinkle with chopped rosemary leaves. Lightly oil the grill rack.

3. Grill your polenta slices over high heat until nicely browned, within 3 to 5 minutes per side.

4. Remove from heat and serve on a heated platter.

139. Griddle Leeks

Preparation Time: 5 minutes
Cooking Time: 15 minutes
Servings: 3
Ingredients:

- 4 leeks (1–1 ½ pounds)
- Salt and pepper, as needed
- Olive oil, as needed

Directions:

1. Heat a griddle over medium to medium-low heat. Trim the root ends of your leeks and cut away the tough green tops.

2. Make a long vertical slit through the center of the leek from the root end through the remaining green part, but not cutting through to the other side. Rinse well to get the sand out from between the layers. Sprinkle both sides with salt.

3. Open up the leeks and place them on the grill directly, cut side down, carefully press down to make sure the layers fan out over the heat.

4. Cook until they have fully softened, 6 to 8 minutes, depending on their thickness. Brush with some oil, turn, and cook until the bottom browns, 1 to 3 minutes.

5. Brush the top using oil, turn, and then cook for another 1 to 3 minutes.

6. Transfer the leeks to a plate, sprinkle with pepper, and serve hot.

140. Grilled Okra

Preparation Time: 5 minutes
Cooking Time: 5–10 minutes
Servings: 3
Ingredients:

- 1 ½ pounds okra pods, stem ends trimmed
- 2 tablespoons good-quality olive oil
- 2 teaspoons coarse sea salt

Directions:

1. Heat a griddle over medium heat. Place the okra in a bowl. Spry with the oil and toss to coat completely. Sprinkle with the salt and toss again.

2. Place the okra on the grill directly. Cook it while turning them once or twice until the pods turn bright green within 5 to 10 minutes.

3. Transfer to your platter and serve hot.

141. Griddle Plum-Tomatoes

Preparation Time: 5 minutes
Cooking Time: 1 hour
Servings: 3
Ingredients:

- 4 plum tomatoes
- Olive oil for brushing

- Salt and pepper, as needed

Directions:

1. Heat a griddle over medium to low indirect heat. Cut the tomatoes in half lengthwise. Brush them with oil and sprinkle the cut sides with salt and pepper.

2. Place the tomatoes on the indirect side of the grill, cut the side up. If the temperature is closer to medium, keep the tomatoes some distance from the heat to avoid charring.

3. Close the grill and cook until wilted, but you can still see signs of moisture, at least 1 hour.

4. About halfway through, move and rotate the tomatoes so they cook evenly.

5. Transfer to your platter and serve hot.

142. Glazed Tofu Steaks with Mango Salsa

Preparation Time: 2 hours
Cooking Time: 5 minutes
Servings: 3
Ingredients:

- 1 bunch fresh cilantro
- 2/3 cup white vegetable stock (below)
- ¼ cup lemon juice
- 1 tablespoon crushed red pepper
- ¼ cup minced fresh ginger
- 1 tablespoon brown sugar
- 1 teaspoon blackstrap molasses
- 5 garlic cloves
- black pepper, to taste
- 1 small fresh pineapple
- 2 mangos
- 1 ¼-pound firm tofu, drained, cut lengthwise into four 1-inch thick steaks
- 1 tablespoon Oil

Directions:

1. Chop the cilantro to make 1/2 cup and set aside 1 tablespoon of it for salsa.

2. Prepare a baking dish, combine the chopped cilantro and the stock, lemon juice, red pepper, ginger, sugar, molasses, garlic, and black pepper. Mix and add the tofu.

3. Marinate it for 2 hours at room temperature. Peel the pineapple and mangos, then finely chop, discard pineapple skin and core, and mango skin and pit.

4. Combine the fruit and 1 tablespoon of the reserved chopped cilantro in a medium serving bowl. Leave to combine flavors. Prepare the outdoor griddle over medium heat. Drain tofu, reserving marinade.

5. Lightly oil the grill and place the tofu over it until lightly browned, 4–5 minutes, frequently brushing with the marinade and turning once. Serve the tofu steaks with the pineapple and mango mixture.

143. Ratatouille

Preparation Time: 15 minutes
Cooking Time: 25 minutes
Servings: 4

Ingredients:

- 1 red onion
- 2 pounds eggplant, sliced into 3/4-inch-thick rounds
- 1 ½ pounds summer squash or zucchini
- 2 bell peppers, stemmed, seeded, and halved, each half cut into thirds
- 1-pound tomatoes, cored and halved
- ¼ cup extra-virgin olive oil (add extra for brushing)
- Salt and pepper, to taste
- 3 tablespoons sherry vinegar
- ¼ cup chopped fresh basil
- 1 tablespoon minced fresh thyme
- 1 garlic clove, minced to paste

Directions:

1. Cut the red onion into 1/2-inch-thick slices and skewer.
2. Cut the zucchini or squash lengthwise and into 1/2-inch-thick planks.
3. Place the onion, eggplant, zucchini, bell peppers, and tomatoes on a baking sheet, brush with oil, and season with salt and pepper. Beat oil, vinegar, basil, thyme, and garlic in a large bowl.
4. Turn all your burners to high, cover, and then heat the grill until hot, within 15 minutes. Next, turn all burners to medium-high.
5. Place the vegetables on the grill and cook, rotating once, until the grill marks, 10 minutes for onion, 10 minutes for eggplant and squash, 7 minutes for peppers, and 5 minutes for tomatoes. Remove vegetables and let cool slightly.
6. Slice the vegetables into 1/2-inch pieces and add to the oil mixture; toss to coat.
7. Season with salt plus pepper to taste and serve warm or at room temperature.

144. Mediterranean Grilled Broccoli

Preparation Time: 1 hour
Cooking Time: 5 minutes
Servings: 3
Ingredients:

- 4 cups broccoli florets
- 1 ½ teaspoon garlic, minced
- 1 ½ teaspoon Italian seasoning
- 1 tablespoon lemon juice
- 4 tablespoons olive oil
- ¼ teaspoons pepper
- 1 ¼ teaspoon kosher salt

Directions:

1. Add broccoli and the remaining ingredients into a bowl and mix well.
2. Cover and place in the refrigerator for 1 hour—preheat the griddle over high heat.
3. Spray the griddle top with cooking spray. Place the broccoli florets on the hot griddle top and cook for 3 minutes on each side.
4. Serve and enjoy.

145. Spinach Salad with Tomato Melts

Preparation Time: 5 minutes
Cooking Time: 6 minutes
Servings: 4
Ingredients:

- 1 or 2 large fresh tomatoes (enough for 4 thick slices across)
- 2 tablespoons good-quality olive oil, plus more for brushing
- Salt and pepper to taste
- 2 teaspoons white wine vinegar
- 1 teaspoon Dijon mustard
- 3 cups baby spinach
- 6 slices cheddar cheese (about 4 ounces)

Directions:

1. Core the tomatoes, cut 4 thick slices (about 1 inch), save the trimmings. Brush them using oil and sprinkle with salt and pepper on both sides.
2. Whisk the 2 tablespoons of oil, vinegar, and mustard together in a bowl.
3. Chop the tomatoes; add them to the dressing along with the spinach and toss until evenly coated.
4. Set the griddle grill to medium-high heat. Oil your griddle and allow it to heat until the oil is shimmering but not smoking. Put the tomato slices and cook for 3 minutes.
5. Turn the tomatoes, top each slice with a slice of cheddar cheese, and cook until the cheese is melted 2 to 3 minutes.
6. Transfer to plates and serve with the salad on top.

146. Eggplant-Wrapped Cantaloupe

Preparation Time: 5 minutes
Cooking Time: 6 minutes
Servings: 8
Ingredients:

- 1 ripe cantaloupe
- Salt and pepper to taste
- 8 thin slices eggplant
- 1 tablespoon Oil

Directions:

1. Cut the cantaloupe lengthwise and get out all the seeds.
2. Cut each half into 8 wedges, and then cut away the rind from each wedge.
3. Put salt and pepper, then wrap each wedge with a slice of eggplant, covering as much of the cantaloupe as possible.
4. Bring the griddle grill to medium-high heat. Oil the griddle and allow it to heat until the oil is shimmering but not smoking.
5. Put the wedges and cook until the eggplant shrivels, and browns in places, 4 to 6 minutes. Serve and enjoy.

147. Wilted Spinach

Preparation Time: 5 minutes
Cooking Time: 1 minute
Servings: 4
Ingredients:

- 8 ounces fresh baby spinach
- 1 tablespoon olive oil
- ¼ teaspoon garlic powder
- ¼ teaspoon salt
- 1 lemon, halved

Directions:

1. Prepare the spinach with olive oil, garlic powder, and salt in a mixing bowl.
2. Bring the griddle grill to medium-high heat. Oil the griddle and allow it to heat until the oil is shimmering but not smoking.

3. Layout the spinach in an even layer and grill for 30 seconds. The leaves should wilt but retain just a bit of crunch.
4. Move to a serving bowl and squeeze a bit of lemon juice on top. Serve immediately.

148. Grilled Yellow Potatoes

Preparation Time: 5 minutes
Cooking Time: 15 minutes
Servings: 4
Ingredients:

- 4 small yellow potatoes
- ¼ olive oil
- ¼ sea salt and black pepper to taste
- ¼ paprika

Directions:

1. Cut the potatoes in half lengthwise and prepare them into a large bag or bowl.
2. Drizzle them with olive oil and stir or shake to coat the potatoes.
3. Add salt, pepper, and paprika to taste, stir, or shake until completely combined.
4. Preheat the griddle grill over medium heat and spray it with oil.
5. Place the potatoes sliced side down, and grill for several minutes or until you can see grill marks and they feel tender on the cut side.
6. Turn the potatoes over and grill until they are tender.
7. Remove from heat and serve.

149. Cauliflower with Garlic and Anchovies

Preparation Time: 10 minutes
Cooking Time: 15 minutes
Servings: 4
Ingredients:

- 1 head cauliflower (1 ½–2 pounds)
- 6 tablespoons good-quality olive oil
- 6 oil-packed anchovy fillets, chopped, or more to taste
- 1 tablespoon minced garlic
- ½ teaspoon red chili flakes (optional)
- Salt and pepper (optional)
- Chopped fresh parsley for garnish

Directions:

1. Break or cut the cauliflower into florets about 1 1/2 inches across; put in a bowl.
2. Put the oil, anchovies, garlic, and red pepper in a small skillet over medium-low heat.
3. Cook, then stir until the anchovies begin to break up, and the garlic begins to color, about 5 minutes.
4. Taste and add more anchovies or some salt and pepper. Add half of the oil mixture over the cauliflower; toss to coat evenly with it.
5. Bring the griddle grill to medium-high heat. Oil the griddle and allow it to heat until the oil is shimmering but not smoking.
6. Put the florets in a single and cook until the cauliflower is as tender and browned as you like it, 5 minutes for crisp-tender to 10 minutes for fully tender.
7. Move to a serving bowl, drizzle over the remaining sauce and the parsley, toss gently, and serve warm or at room temperature.

150. Watermelon Steaks with Rosemary

Preparation Time: 10 minutes
Cooking Time: 10 minutes
Servings: 4
Ingredients:

- 1 small watermelon
- ¼ cup good-quality olive oil
- 1 tablespoon minced fresh rosemary
- Salt and pepper to taste
- Lemon wedges for serving

Directions:

1. Cut the watermelon into 2-inch-thick slices, with the rind intact, and then into halves or quarters, if you like. If there are seeds, use a fork to remove as many as you can without tearing up the flesh too much.
2. Put the oil and rosemary in a small bowl, sprinkle with salt and pepper, and stir.
3. Massage the mixture all over the watermelon slices. (You can prepare the watermelon for the grill up to 2 hours ahead; wrap it in plastic tightly to keep it from drying out and refrigerate.)

4. Bring the griddle grill to medium-high heat. Oil the griddle and allow it to heat until the oil is shimmering but not smoking.

5. Put the watermelon on the griddle and cook, turning once, until the flesh develops grill marks and has dried out a bit, 4 to 5 minutes per side.

6. Transfer to a platter and serve with lemon wedges.

151. Grilled Summer Squash

Preparation Time: 5 minutes
Cooking Time: 10 minutes
Servings: 12
Ingredients:

- 1 summer squash
- 2 tablespoons olive oil
- Sea salt to taste

Directions:

1. Slice the squash in half lengthwise.
2. Add oil to the squash and season with salt.
3. Heat the griddle grill over medium heat and set the squash cut side down.
4. Cook for 5 minutes per side until it is tender.

5. Remove from heat and serve.

152. Grilled Brussels Sprouts with Balsamic Glaze

Preparation Time: 5 minutes
Cooking Time: 10 minutes
Servings: 4
Ingredients:

- 1 pound medium Brussels sprouts
- 4 tablespoons olive oil
- Sea salt to taste
- ¼ cup balsamic vinegar

Directions:

1. Cut the sprouts in half lengthwise from top to bottom.
2. Brush with olive oil and season with sea salt.
3. Bring the griddle grill to medium-high heat. Oil the griddle and allow it to heat until the oil is shimmering but not smoking.
4. Grill the sprouts cut side down for 5 minutes on each side.
5. Brush the sprouts lightly with balsamic, grill for a minute or so more to set the vinegar before serving.

CONCLUSION

A quality outdoor gas griddle is designed to be weather resistant and can be used with propane or natural gas. It is made with a non-stick surface that allows for quick release and easy cleanup.

Good things about this gas griddle include its durability, which is brought by its heavy-duty cast iron body. The square shape of the cooking areas allows you to cook a lot of food simultaneously. Also, it is easy to move from one place to another.

When cooking with gas, there are some things you have to consider. First of all, gas griddles have high temperatures. It means that you cannot touch the metal when it is hot. To prevent getting burned by this device, use a low flame or stainless-steel pot to prepare food. Secondly, do not stick the spatula in the flame as it can cause burns and accidents. Lastly, only turn on the gas when it is cold.

Gas griddles have many advantages that you can use to make your life easier and more convenient. It can make a lot of difference in your lifestyle. You can use them for cooking healthy meals, and you do not have to worry about the same oil used in other cooking methods. Cooking in a gas griddle is also a good way to save money because fewer expenses are involved. You only have to buy the materials you need for your recipes.

You will be able to increase the number of healthy foods you eat by using a gas griddle. You will be delighted to find that you do not have to compromise your food quality because of this device. It is one of the reasons why people prefer gas griddles to other types.

Using a gas griddle does not only make your recipes appealing, but it also helps you prepare healthy food. The answer is that a gas griddle cooks faster and allows you to control the temperature for your recipes to come out just right. The secret is all about cooking at the proper temperatures and in the right amounts. It allows you to cook good meals with less or healthier oil.

When it comes to cooking with gas griddles, there are a lot of options you could choose from. It is because they come in different varieties. Nonetheless, you can still prepare healthy foods. The trick is to choose the right one for your recipe.

The recipes in this guide will help you get the hang of incorporating gas griddles in your cooking. You will learn how to use them and what different recipes you can prepare using a gas griddle.

While various qualities can be found in gas griddles, there is only one quality that matters—how you will use it. Your gas griddles should be used for cooking the types of foods that you like and enjoy. If these are your needs and desires, then this product would be a good investment for you. With this being said, make sure to look for the best gas griddle to get the most out of it.

With all these things considered, we can conclude that gas griddles are indeed a great investment for your kitchen. You can consider them for their versatility, ease of use, and the food you can cook with them. Now that you know more about these outdoor griddles, it is time to have one in your kitchen to prepare great food for every meal of the day. After all, it is always nice to have a gas griddle in your kitchen to make food even better.

Made in United States
Troutdale, OR
06/17/2024

20621825R00060